AROUND THE
MED

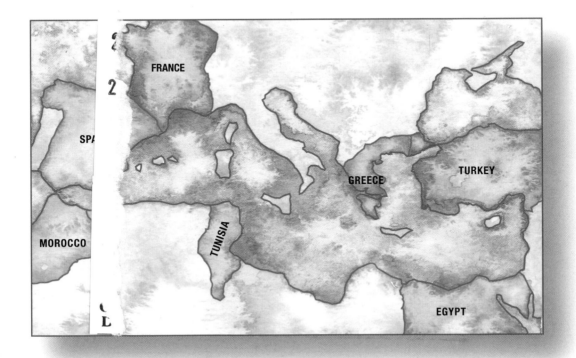

AROUND THE
MED

Keith Floyd

HarperCollins*Illustrated*

First published in 2000 by HarperCollins*Illustrated*
an imprint of HarperCollins*Publishers*.

Text © Keith Floyd 2000

Photographs p.50 bottom, p.64, p.94 bottom, p.122,
p.123 top, p.124 © Mike Connor 1999

All other location photographs of Keith Floyd and food
photographs © HarperCollins*Publishers* 2000

All other location photographs © Kim Sayer 2000

Channel 5 logos are trademarks of Channel 5 Broadcasting
Limited and © Channel 5 Broadcasting Limited 2000

Keith Floyd is represented by Stan Green Management,
Dartmouth, Devon; telephone 01803 770046;
fax 01803 770075. Visit **www.keithfloyd.co.uk**
The Channel 5 TV series 'Floyd around the Med' is produced
by Denham Productions.

Location photography: Kim Sayer, Mike Connor
Food photography: Michelle Garrett
Home Economist: Joanna Farrow
Editor: Jane Middleton
Designer: Liz Brown
Indexer: Susan Bosanko

A catalogue record for this book is available from
the British Library

ISBN 0 00 414087 7
Colour origination and printing by Bath Press.

right Old Cataract Hotel, Aswan, Egypt;

the view from Agatha Christie's suite.

contents

INTRODUCTION

The primary flavours of the Mediterranean are olive oil, thyme, rosemary, basil, garlic and saffron. The main vegetables are aubergines, peppers, tomatoes and courgettes. All these are overlaid with a mist of lemon, nuts and spices from the East – nutmeg, cumin, cinnamon, cardamom, coriander, turmeric, chilli flakes, sea salt, black pepper, caraway and others. Rice, pasta, pulses and grains are preferred to the potato. Artichokes, spinach, celery leaves and mint are mixed with crunchy greens for salads.

But the Mediterranean, which laps the shores of Europe, Asia and Africa, is populated by Christians, Arabs and Jews, by Latins and Moors, some meat eaters, some vegetarians, some pork lovers, and some nut lovers. Some of the countries are highly developed and have refrigerators and microwaves; others have simple clay pots with a few glowing embers of charcoal. Irrespective of creed, culture and cash, everyone shares a common love of food, whether it be fish, goat, lamb, pigeons and all manner of fowl, or fruit.

The recipes in this book are authentic, although I have modified some. Many of them come from cooks who have never seen a television cookery show or read a cookery book. Indeed, many of them cannot read. They have never weighed or measured an ingredient in their lives, and may well time the cooking from the cockerel's early-morning alarm call to the moment the shadow falls over the pigsty. As a consequence, these recipes require the reader to apply simple common sense to the quantities, the sizes of pots, the volume of liquid and the length of time things take to cook. Remember, this is not a workshop manual. Cooking is not a science. Cooking is a way of demonstrating your appreciation of nature and making a gift of kindness and love to those whose company you enjoy. And the love of good food, generosity and hospitality is central to the Mediterranean people's way of life which, like olive oil, that indispensable liquid that flavours, cooks and heals, is as old as time and civilization, whether you are squatting on a rush mat in a hut on the banks of the River Nile or dining in the ornate splendour of Monte Carlo.

Note on the recipes

In most of the recipes in this book, quantities and timings are approximate. The style of cooking in the countries around the Mediterranean is completely different from that of northern Europe. People tend to live in extended families, and so they cook for eight to ten people. There is not a cook in the Mediterranean area who would give you a recipe for, let's say, moussaka, or beef stifado, for four people. They simply make up a pot of the stuff, with enough ingredients to go round. Any left over would be reheated and served the next day.

It is important to note that the recipes in this book are not 'dinner-party dishes'. Although they are all prepared with love and the freshest ingredients, they are a casual, everyday part of Mediterranean life. Family or guests invited to a birthday or a Sunday family reunion will not be expecting a formal four-course meal followed by coffee and mints. Right, having said all that, I will repeat myself, just to be on the safe side: common sense must be applied to the quantities, cooking times and serving of these dishes. Finally, every time a recipe requires olive oil, this means olive oil. There is no substitute for it if you wish the dish to taste authentic – except where I suggest peanut, sesame or walnut oil!

Mezze, moussaka & myths

There is much more to Greek cooking than moussaka, stuffed vine leaves, greasy kebabs stuffed into pitta bread pockets with chips, salad and mayonnaise, and the ubiquitous Greek salad with a slab of feta cheese sprinkled with dried oregano. This may be what most of us encounter on our Greek holidays but if you search around a bit you will discover some very fine dishes indeed. Take the aubergine, for example. It's essential in a moussaka but there's much more to it than that. You could write a whole book about cooking aubergines the Greek way. They can be made into a wonderfully refreshing salad, or stuffed with minced mutton or lamb and roasted in the oven, or deep-fried in batter, or fried in olive oil and served cold with a marinade of lemon juice, finely chopped garlic and parsley, coriander, fennel or dill. Courgettes can be given the same agreeable treatment as aubergines, and vegetables à la grecque (cooked in a lemon and olive oil marinade) are really most enjoyable. Baby vegetables such as leeks, onions and artichoke hearts can all be cooked in the same way as mushrooms à la grecque (see page 15).

In Greece they love to cook with fresh herbs, such as coriander, dill, parsley, mint and spring onions, combined with lemon juice (I swear that Greek lemons produce some of the finest juice I have ever encountered). They like to use coriander seeds and cinnamon to flavour their dishes, and occasionally cumin. At its best, Greek cooking is light, refreshing, tasty and tangy – for example, lamb stewed with Cos lettuce or green peas, flavoured with a wonderful lemon sauce, is an exquisite dish. Stuffed vine leaves (see page 18) don't have to be briny, vinegary things with congealed rice inside. Like cabbage leaves, they can be stuffed delightfully with a mixture of rice, fish or meat, maybe pine nuts, sultanas or currants.

chicken with lemons
and raisins

In this dish, which is really a simple chicken cooked in tomato sauce, we can see the influence that the Moors have had on Mediterranean cooking by the use of fruits and spices.

1	free range chicken (how heavy? I hear you cry! Well, I don't know. If there are 2–4 of you, get a small one; more of you, get a great big one or two small ones! If the chicken has its liver and heart, so much the better)
	olive oil
2	onions, finely diced
4	fat cloves of garlic, very finely crushed
about ½ bottle	white wine
about 500ml/ 18fl oz	tomato sauce (buy this in a carton)
4	juicy lemons, cut in half, pips removed, then very, very, very finely sliced
1	cinnamon stick
about 225g/8oz	raisins, currants or sultanas
1	sprig of thyme
4–5	cloves
	sea salt and black pepper

Joint the chicken, bones and all, into manageable morsels. In a large, shallow sauté pan or a deep frying pan, heat up some olive oil. The pan needs to be big enough to hold all the pieces of chicken in a single layer. Fry them on both sides until golden brown, then add the onions and garlic and brown them very lightly. At this stage, if you have the giblets from the chicken, add them and fry them too. Now pour in the wine so that it half covers the chicken and boil furiously until it has reduced, then add enough tomato sauce just to cover the chicken. Keep on cooking for a few minutes, then add the lemons, cinnamon, raisins, thyme and cloves. By now, since the chicken went into the pan, it will have been cooking for about 25 minutes. Stir the whole lot together and let it simmer gently until the chicken is tender and you have a fragrant, spicy, lemon-tanged tomato sauce.

I am not the kind of cook who offers (quote) serving suggestions (unquote!). It is up to you, but I think pasta, rice, vermicelli or salad would be good with this. Because, you see, this kind of dish, which is cooked with vegetables and fruit, just doesn't need a plate of carrots, green beans or similar, next to it. A few chips and olive oil might be quite nice, however!

A NOTE ON HERBS
As a general rule, branches of dried herbs such as thyme and rosemary work best when barbecuing and grilling because they are cooked into the overall flavour; they are also very good in casseroles and stews that require long cooking. However, when the herb is used as an edible garnish (i.e. not cooked) or only cooked very lightly, fresh herbs are essential.

fricassée of spring lamb
with green peas and egg and lemon sauce

Egg and lemon sauce, known as *avgolemono*, is served with vegetables, meat, chicken and fish throughout Greece. Since this is a spring dish it is essential that the lamb is young and fresh, not frozen. Throughout the Mediterranean, this fricassée would be prepared with milk-fed lamb at best and, at worst, meat from a very, very young sheep.

SERVES 6

about 1.5–2kg/ 3¼–4½lb	leg of spring lamb (you might have to buy 1½ legs)
175g/6oz	unsalted butter
500g/1lb 2oz	baby leeks (the thickness of your average fountain pen), the white and green parts cut into 4cm/1½ inch batons
½	hearty, dark-green Cos (romaine) lettuce, ripped into rough pieces
1.5kg/3¼lb	small frozen peas (yes, frozen, because unless you have access to the tenderest of fresh garden peas, this dish will be ruined by those tough old things the size of golf balls, so-called fresh garden peas from the average greengrocer; also, frozen peas contain their own moisture)
1	bunch of fresh dill or coriander, or parsley or even chives, chopped
	sea salt and black pepper

FOR THE SAUCE:

1 heaped tbsp	butter
1 tbsp	plain flour
juice of 5 or 6	lemons (possibly less if you are making this on holiday where lemons grow; possibly more if you are using the slightly less juicy ones at home)
2	eggs and
4	egg yolks

Cut the lamb off the bone into nice bite-sized pieces. Melt half the butter in a cast-iron, copper or other heavy-based wide casserole and fry the lamb pieces until they are browned on all sides. Because it is spring lamb it will not take very long to cook, so just brown it lightly. Then stir in the leeks and cook for a few minutes to soften them a little. Throw in the roughly torn up lettuce, then the frozen (yes, still frozen) peas and fresh herbs. Add one or two cups of water and the remaining butter, then season with salt and pepper. Stir the whole lot round so everything is combined, put the lid on and simmer gently for about 30–45 minutes. Inspect and taste the dish from time to time to make sure that the peas are defrosting, the lamb is cooking and all the juices are amalgamating.

When you think the lamb is almost cooked, strain off about a cupful of the cooking liquid, leaving only a small amount in the pan. Now, in a separate heavy-based pan, make the sauce. Melt the butter, add the flour and whisk well, so that you have a golden, but not burnt, roux. Whisk in the cooking liquid you have taken from the lamb and peas until you have a thick, smooth sauce. Now, over a low heat whisk in some lemon juice until it has

almost the consistency of custard. In a jug, lightly whisk together the eggs and egg yolks. With the heat switched off, gradually add the beaten eggs to the sauce, whisking furiously, until you have what does, in fact, look like custard. If the pan is too hot or you whisk too slowly, you will curdle the whole thing, so do be careful.

Put the lamb and peas on to a serving platter and pour over the egg and lemon sauce.

In the South of France salads of dandelion leaves are common but in Greece dandelions are more likely to be stir-fried with wonderful olive oil, lemon juice, cinnamon and salt and pepper. The bitterness of the leaves is mellowed by the sweetness of the oil and spiked with the cinnamon and lemon juice.

It is quite hard to find these dishes properly cooked. Although the Greeks have all these wonderful recipes there don't appear to be many people interested in producing them. The basic taverna idea is a good one: a dozen or so stews, soups or ragouts, plus a selection of vegetable dishes, are cooked in the morning and kept warm all day in a bain marie. This means quick eating, plus you can see what you're getting, but by the evening the dishes tend to be a little stale and overcooked. A good tip is to eat in tavernas at lunchtime but in the evenings go to places that cook to order on the barbecue. In this way you can enjoy barbecued octopus or a variety of fresh fish or shellfish or excellent – sometimes – lamb *souvlakia* (kebabs), or offal kebabs, or freshly cooked minced meat balls and delicate, tiny lamb chops simply grilled and eaten with a squeeze of lemon juice.

Of course, one of the great joys of eating in Greece is when you come across a restaurant or bar that takes trouble over its mezze. These are the Greek hors d'oeuvre, or the Greek *tapas* if you wish. The ancient Greeks claimed to have invented mezze, although visitors to Athens thought it was just an excuse for the Athenians' miserliness. The ancient Greek writer Lyceus reckoned an Athenian dinner was an insult. He felt affronted to be offered five or six small plates, one with garlic, another with some sea urchins or a little piece of marinated fish or a few cockles, possibly a few olives. But it was the beginning. Today, of course, mezze can be truly pleasing. At its simplest it might be a bowl of pickled vegetables such as carrots, chillies or cauliflower and a dish of nutty, delicious olives, or it might be a mini feast of vegetables à la grecque or little filo pastry pockets filled with cream cheese and spinach, or tzatziki – a wonderfully refreshing yoghurt dip – or stuffed vine leaves, or the oddly named aubergine salad, which is in

below Olives are indispensable to the Mediterranean table.

fact a beautiful purée of baked aubergines, or taramosalata which, sadly, throughout Greece is pretty insipid, artificially coloured goo. You'll find my recipe (see page 17) much better than anything you will eat in Greece – ha! Or raw fish marinated with lemon juice and olive oil, or just little pieces of marinated grilled octopus. Much of Greek cooking is done by rule of thumb and experience rather than by careful measuring. Greeks (like most Mediterranean people) don't cook dinner parties for two, or four, or six, like people in northern Europe do. They cook as much as the dish will hold for as many people as they think can eat it. So you must, I warn you, when you attempt any of these recipes bear in mind that all measurements, times and weights are approximate. Please use common sense.

mezze (Greek hors d'oeuvre)

mushrooms à la grecque

750g/1lb 10oz	very small mushrooms (the size of an average olive)
juice of 4	lemons
	olive oil
1	large onion, very finely diced
750g/1lb 10oz	tomatoes, skinned, deseeded and finely diced
1 level tbsp	of equal quantities of crushed peppercorns and coriander seeds
2 or 3	bay leaves
1	sprig of thyme
1 tbsp	tomato purée
1	bunch of fresh coriander, chopped
	sea salt

First, clean the mushrooms if necessary – if you decide to wash them, make sure you dry them very carefully – then marinate them in the lemon juice for 10–15 minutes.

Secondly, heat some olive oil in a shallow sauté pan or a large, deep frying pan, add the onion and tomatoes and fry swiftly for a minute or two. Then add the peppercorns and coriander seeds, bay leaves, thyme, tomato purée and possibly a dash of water. Bring to the boil and simmer for a few minutes until you have a nice tangy sauce. Now add the mushrooms and lemon juice and cook for 5–6 minutes more or until the mushrooms are cooked and the sauce has reduced a little. Add salt to taste. Tip into a serving dish. When cool, chill in the refrigerator. Serve with chopped coriander leaves sprinkled over.

The mushrooms will be even better tomorrow than today.

cream cheese and spinach in filo pastry

The Greeks love these little triangular, puffed, savoury pastries. They are very easy to make and you can use any kind of filling you like. For example, spicy minced lamb in a thick tomato sauce with coriander and chillies; purée of salt cod; or cooked, chopped courgettes instead of spinach. The minced lamb filling would be good with a bowl of that much-loved Greek yoghurt dish, tzatziki (see opposite).

900g/2lb	fresh spinach
	a large knob of butter
	grated nutmeg
225g/8oz	top-quality cream cheese
3	eggs
3 tbsp	chopped fresh mint
1 packet	filo pastry
	melted butter for brushing
	a little beaten egg to glaze
	sesame seeds
	sea salt and black pepper

Cook the spinach with the butter and no water whatsoever in a pan with a lid. Leave to cool, then strain off the liquid and chop the spinach finely. Season with salt and pepper and a little nutmeg. Beat together the cream cheese and eggs, then mix this with the spinach and mint.

To make each pastry, take a sheet of filo pastry and cut a strip about 10 x 20cm/4 x 8 inches. Lay it on a work surface and brush with melted butter. Before you add the filling, turn the top left-hand edge of the pastry over to meet the right-hand straight side (this forms the triangular shape), then unfold it. The mark left will show you where to put the filling. Place a tablespoon of the filling to the right side, refold the corner and seal the edges. Repeat the triangular folding until you have a complete packet. Brush with beaten egg, sprinkle with sesame seeds, place on a buttered baking tray and bake for about 30 minutes in an oven preheated to 200°C/400°F/Gas Mark 6. Serve hot or cold.

tzatziki

This wonderfully refreshing sauce, dip, starter, call it what you will, is very versatile. It can be used as an accompaniment to simple lamb *souvlakia* (kebabs), spread on little squares of bread as a snack with your apéritif, or served as a dip to go with mixed, raw vegetables (crudités) such as crisp batons of carrot, celery, spring onion etc.

1	cucumber, unpeeled
500g/1lb 2oz	best-quality Greek yoghurt
6	garlic cloves, very finely chopped, then crushed into a paste
	olive oil
	wine vinegar
	sea salt

Cut the cucumber lengthways in half, remove the seeds with a teaspoon and discard. Grate the cucumber on a cheese grater, put into a colander and sprinkle with sea salt. Leave to drain for 30 minutes–1 hour. Give it a good shake to make it as dry as possible.

Put the yoghurt into a bowl, whisk in the garlic paste and add the cucumber. Stir in well, then stir in a dash of olive oil and a dash of vinegar. Taste it and add a little more olive oil and vinegar if necessary (it must not be too runny). Refrigerate until required.

taramosalata

It is hard to find good taramosalata even in Greece. It is invariably made with anonymous fish roe, potatoes, ordinary oil and pink colouring and is, quite frankly, revolting! My version is expensive, excellent and simple.
As with all the preceding mezze, this goes well with nicely charred, grilled pitta bread. It will taste even better if you can toast it over a charcoal grill.

2	fat cloves of garlic, peeled
100g/4oz	smoked cod's roe – the best has the skin still attached, which needs to be painstakingly peeled off
	finest-quality olive oil
	lemon juice
	some fine, fresh white breadcrumbs

First purée the garlic in a food processor, then add the cod's roe little by little until they are combined. As the food processor goes whizzing around, slowly and evenly pour in a thin stream of olive oil until you have a smooth paste. Next add some lemon juice to taste. Switch off the machine; you may find some olive oil has floated to the top. Switch on the machine again and add some breadcrumbs, a few at a time, until the excess oil has been absorbed.

17

stuffed vine leaves

Because these are fiddly to prepare, and because they are best eaten cold, it is wise to make them the day before you plan to eat them.

You could add finely minced lamb or beef to the filling, cooked with a little tomato sauce like a dry bolognese sauce.

Blanch the vine leaves a few at a time in lightly salted boiling water, then cool them in a bowl of cold water. Drain and lay out flat on a work surface.

Mix together all the remaining ingredients except the lemon juice and tomato passata, adding a dash of olive oil. Place a small amount of the mixture on each leaf, turn in the sides and then roll them into little sausage shapes. Next, coat the base of a large saucepan with olive oil and cover the bottom with spare vine leaves, unfolded. Then arrange the stuffed vine leaves in circles to cover the bottom of the pan and build up layers until you have used them all up. Add the lemon juice and enough water just to cover the vine rolls. Find a plate or bowl that fits exactly inside the saucepan. Put this on top of the vine rolls to stop them floating up during the cooking process.

Bring to the boil and then simmer gently until the liquid has disappeared and the rice is practically cooked. If there is any liquid left at this stage, carefully strain it off. Now add the tomato sauce and continue to simmer until the rice is fully cooked. Leave to cool and then refrigerate overnight in the saucepan (do not attempt to turn them out while they are warm as they will break up into a shambolic mess!).

Next day, arrange the stuffed vine leaves on a serving dish in a single layer and pour the sauce over. Grind some coarse black pepper over the lot and serve with wedges of lemon.

50–60	vine leaves (available in vacuum packs or, if you are lucky, loose in brine from a good specialist food shop)
2	large onions, finely chopped
1	bunch of peppery spring onions, very finely chopped.
1	good bunch of fresh dill, very finely chopped
1	bunch of fresh mint, finely chopped
1½ cups	rice, well rinsed, drained and dried
	olive oil
juice of 4	lemons
500ml/18fl oz	tomato passata
	sea salt and black pepper
	lemon wedges, to serve

marinated fish

Here's one for those of you who happen to like a spot of fishing. If you catch a couple of fish, it doesn't matter what sort they are at all (of course, you can buy fish from the fishmonger, ho, ho, ho!). But remember that the fish must be very fresh, since it isn't cooked.

Fillet and skin the fish. Cut the fillets into bite-sized pieces, wash them and dry very carefully. Put them into a shallow earthenware or similar dish, squeeze over some lemon juice and add a dash of white wine vinegar so that the fish is half covered. Chuck in some finely chopped garlic, a couple of crushed peppercorns, a couple of very finely chopped chillies and a dash of olive oil, plus a bit of salt and pepper. Leave in the fridge for one hour and then turn the fish over to marinate the other side. Leave it in the fridge for a minimum of 4 hours (preferably overnight). Serve with fresh bread. The fish is raw but 'cooked' by the marinade.

aubergine salad

Another dish that benefits from being prepared the day before as it needs to be chilled and, anyway, the flavours mature nicely this way. Serve spread on cubes of country bread as part of a mezze.

6	aubergines
2–3 tbsp	tahini (sesame paste)
	lemon juice to taste (at least 2 lemons)
about 4 tbsp	olive oil
6	tomatoes, skinned, deseeded and finely diced (to skin them, drop them into rapidly boiling water for a few seconds; the skins will break and they will be easy to peel)
2	spicy spring onions, very finely diced
1	bunch of fresh coriander, very finely chopped
	sea salt and black pepper

Dry-roast the aubergines in a very hot oven until the skins are blackened and charred. Leave to cool. Cut them in half, scrape out the pulp and drain through a fine sieve to extract any remaining moisture. Put the strained aubergine pulp and the tahini into a food processor and whizz to a coarse purée. Tip into a bowl and whisk in some lemon juice and olive oil (it should not be too runny). Then stir in the tomatoes, spring onions and coriander and season to taste. Chill overnight.

POSTCARDS FROM GREECE

Corfu, April

The journey to Corfu, our first destination in Greece, was miserable. We got to Malaga airport at about 7am with two huge tin trunks full of all my cooking equipment, only to find we had to pay about £700 in excess baggage. Then we discovered that the trunks could not be booked through to Corfu because we had to fly from Malaga to Madrid, Madrid to Athens and Athens to Corfu, and there were no porters in Malaga or Madrid. If we had had to unload the trunks we could not possibly have shifted them. It took four of us to get them on the plane in the first place. However, we finally made it to Corfu at about 1 o'clock the next morning, the Greek Orthodox Easter Saturday, only to find that it was absolutely freezing. We had expected weather similar to Spain and had packed accordingly. To make matters worse we were checked into the most appalling excuse for a hotel I have ever seen in my life. It had no bar, no lift, no lights, the lavatory ran incessantly, the taps dripped and the beds were slatted wooden affairs with thin sponge mattresses. There were no power points, no services or facilities of any kind, except for a breakfast of stale bread and jam plus dreadful coffee made from ground roasted acorns. I can tell you we were feeling very sorry for ourselves, and to make matters worse everybody in the pub before we left had said, 'Oh, you don't want to go to Corfu, it's full of lager louts!' I was very much in mind of Bob Dylan's song, 'You're lost in worries, it's raining and it's Eastertime too.'

below It never rains but it pours.

I had a cooking sketch to do that afternoon but because a huge Easter procession was planned, all the shops were shut. Acquiring food was really quite difficult, and trying to buy pullovers and waterproof jackets was a problem, which luckily my wife, Tess, overcame.

In between downpours the sun shone brightly, while a very cold wind, which blew in from Albania just a couple of miles across the water, whistled through the narrow back streets of Corfu Old Town. We weren't due to start filming until about 11 o'clock, so we wandered about the streets and discovered that the Old Town is a charming place: wonderful Venetian architecture, cheerful cafés, bars and restaurants, and an absurd concrete cricket pitch set in the middle of the park for the expats.

As it got closer to 11 o'clock the streets, which at 9 o'clock had been completely empty, began to fill with people – first a few hundred, then a few thousand, then tens of thousands – all lining the route for the grand procession that was to take place to celebrate the resurrection of Christ. In cynical mood, I took my place in the jostling crowds, waiting without any enthusiasm whatsoever for the band to begin to play – some shambolic, out-of-step, scruffy group of people in motley uniforms, banging drums and missing notes on trumpets, I assumed. But to my great delight and excitement I was completely wrong.

The parade was spectacular. The first band came into view and into earshot through a very narrow street, fanning out as the street widened. Its members were dressed immaculately in blue and gold uniforms with polished silver helmets, and playing the most moving music – classical in style but presumably religious. They were succeeded by sombre-looking priests dressed in black with curious stove-pipe hats, flanking a man, berobed but not of the cloth, as it were, who was carrying a huge crucifix draped with a picture of Christ. Then came more processions – of priests, a female choir, scouts, girl guides and children in neat white socks, blue pullovers and blue shorts, and more bands – some dressed in crimson and again playing spectacularly moving music.

above Pot throwing during the Easter Parade in Old Corfu.

It took an hour for the entire musical procession to pass where I stood, and as it fanned out into the wider street the crowd moved in behind it, following it round to the cathedral. After the service, the citizens of Corfu celebrated the Christian resurrection with a pagan ritual. In the times of the ancient Greeks, whenever someone died a member of the family would stay behind as the body was taken away and, as the cortege moved off, would throw an earthenware pot from the house so that it smashed on to the street, warding away evil spirits from the dead and bringing good fortune to the bereaved. Today, of course, this is just a piece of folklore but it's mightily impressive. Many of the houses in the Old Town are three or four storeys high, all with balconies. Everybody gathers on their balconies and hurls huge clay pots on to the road below. I was doing a piece to camera, pretending to be a famous war correspondent explaining this ritual, when I was actually saved by a Greek policeman who rugby-tackled me out of the path of a down-coming missile. It was damned funny! The crew enjoyed it.

For the next 24 hours, virtually every street in Old Corfu was covered in shattered clay pots. It was like walking on a gravel beach and was hugely good fun. And the sun was shining now, and it really was a pretty place. I believe there were 40,000 people in the streets that day, all crossing themselves as the various parts of the procession passed, and virtually all of them were Greek. The celebration was no cheapskate performance put on for tourists; it was done out of deep belief and

longheld tradition.

We broke for lunch and I found a little taverna opposite a vegetable shop that had just opened – luckily, so I could buy food for my cooking sketch. It was a curious restaurant, openfronted, very friendly but they didn't have a kitchen. All the food came from a sort of shed down an alleyway. We had a wonderful plate of grilled octopus, shrimps and sardines and, as it turned out, the only good moussaka that I was to eat on my whole trip. Really delicate, fresh, finely minced lamb topped with a light, cinnamon-flavoured béchamel sauce and served with a crunchy salad of sweet onions, tomatoes, excellent olive oil and good feta cheese. It was delightful and our spirits were high because the procession had been so dramatic – full of pathos yet also a celebration.

That evening there was another Mass, and at 11 o'clock the priests, maybe 120 of them, sort of marched, sort of shambled, sort of glided even, from the church to the bandstand in the park, where all of the bands from the morning were gathered. After a blessing on the tens of thousands of people present, the bands began to play and the music was simply fantastic. Then, as one, they stopped and at that moment a huge red crucifix was switched on, high up on the hill. Simultaneously the night sky erupted in explosions of brilliant fireworks.

below A priest relaxes, while awaiting the Easter parade.

We returned to our hotel at 1am, having moved from the fleapit we'd been in to the quite excellent Corfu Palace Hotel. It was serving an Easter dinner for 400 guests of what can only be described as haggis soup, a traditional Greek Easter soup made from the pluck of lamb (the liver, lungs and heart) and pearl barley or oatmeal. We slept very badly in this luxurious and comfortable hotel because outside our bedroom windows, all through the night, men were building a huge barbecue. After the religious services of Good Friday and Easter Saturday, Easter Sunday is given over to feasting on barbecued whole lambs, symbolic of the innocence of Jesus. A curious thing, religion: a lamb represents innocence and piety so it is killed and eaten.

In the morning we trundled off to a small, higgledy-piggledy village in the extreme south of the island, with tatty houses brightly painted in purple, vermilion, yellow and white. In the muddy communal squares in front of the houses the entire village was occupied in barbecuing lambs. There were probably about 150 people and 30 or 40 lambs. Barbecuing is something that many people don't really understand. The coals underneath these lambs were quite small, whereas we Brits tend to light a huge, raging fire. In fact I was once told in Africa that an African in the bush would light a small fire and stand close to it whereas a white man would light a huge fire and stand away from it – think about it! Of course, in the village they had – as everybody should have when barbecuing – two fires. You light your first fire and let the wood burn down until you have grey, dust-covered coals which give off immense heat. Meanwhile, you light another fire so that when the one on which you are barbecuing begins to diminish you can just add more coals from the second fire.

above Barbecuing – the Greek way.

Gnarled old men and young children alike squatted at these spits just a foot or two above the ground, all holding umbrellas and makeshift corrugated iron roofs over them because by this time it was tipping down with rain. The village priest came up, clutching a large jar of moonshine, and offered us all a drink. Wine in five-litre jars was flowing liberally and the aroma emanating from the wonderful spring lambs was just mouthwatering. It was, despite the rain, a seriously splendid day.

Afterwards we drove cheerfully in our open-topped car along the narrow lanes, which were a riot of colour – yellow and blue wild flowers, blossoming bougainvillea and carpets of pink flowering marjoram. As we passed through little hamlets and villages the embers of the barbecues were still smoking slightly and the air was redolent with roast lamb and sweet-smelling pine.

Athens, Tuesday

When you consider that Greek architects created masterpieces 500 years before the birth of Christ you have to ask yourself what's gone wrong. Athens is an absolute dump. The Old Town, the Plaka, is OK, with pretty squares and charming little restaurants, but the rest is just a massive traffic jam under a canopy of smog. I don't know why my friends tell me that Athens is a great place to visit. I certainly didn't find it so. I did the obligatory trip up the Acropolis and learnt a lot about it in 10 minutes flat – for example, that it's called the Acropolis because it's in the highest part of town. Any important town in ancient Greece would have had an Acropolis. This particular one is dedicated to Athena, the goddess of wisdom. She must have been some goddess because she emanated from the head of Zeus fully grown and fully armed. In a battle with some giants, she picked up the island of Sicily and flattened them with it. I like things like that!

Wandering around the Plaka, which is full of gift shops and restaurants, is a bit frustrating, because although the food looks quite nice you quickly get fed up with being touted by smart-suited head waiters handing out cards and menus. Yep, all in all I have to say that my three or four days' sojourn in Athens was roughly three or four days too long.

sauté of spring lamb **with apricots**

	olive oil
1.5kg/3¼ lb	boneless shoulder or leg of spring lamb, cut into 2.5cm/1 inch cubes (leave any fat on)
2	onions, finely diced
8	garlic cloves, finely chopped
6	large tomatoes, skinned, deseeded and finely chopped
4 tbsp	tomato purée
1	sprig of thyme
juice of 4	lemons
225g/8oz	dried apricots, cut in half
1	bunch of fresh mint, chopped (sundried mint has more flavour and is possibly better than fresh in this instance; use half the quantity)
1	large tub of Greek yoghurt
1	bunch of fresh coriander, chopped
	sea salt and black pepper

Heat some olive oil in a shallow sauté pan or deep frying pan and fry the lamb until it is golden brown. Now add the onions, garlic and tomatoes and fry until the onions begin to colour very lightly. Stir in the tomato purée. Add the thyme, lemon juice, apricots, mint and seasoning and simmer for about an hour, until the meat is tender. If after, say, 10 minutes, the dish looks a little dry, add a drop of water or, if you have it, lamb or chicken stock.

Serve with a dollop of yoghurt and a sprinkling of fresh coriander.

A really good vegetable to go with this is a purée of aubergines. All you need to do is preheat your oven to the highest level and dry-roast some aubergines in it until charred and blackened. When they are cool, cut them open and scrape out the pulp. Mash the pulp, put it in a saucepan and heat gently. Stir in some double cream, season with salt, pepper and cinnamon and then sprinkle in (stirring all the while) some good-quality instant potato until you have a thick, smooth, creamy purée; you could possibly whisk in a knob of butter, too.

Santorini, Saturday

I was delighted to set off to the island of Santorini in the Cyclades, just a one-hour flight from Athens. And, to quote the *Michelin Green Guide*: 'The island of Santorini, the southernmost of the larger Cyclades, is one of the most spectacular in the Mediterranean. It presents an awesome sight with volcanic craters partly submerged by the sea. It is particularly impressive to approach by boat' – which I did, and then had a spectacular mule ride up 587 zigzag steps that cling precariously to the edge of the precipitous rocks leading to the little town. It is beautiful – narrow, cobbled streets, breathtaking views across the turquoise sea, spectacular sunsets – and produces excellent white wine. The interesting thing is, because it's such a windswept island, they grow their vines in little low

circles like garlands or Christmas wreaths, and all the grapes form inside the circle. This way they're protected from the fierce winds and, because there's very little water on Santorini, any natural humidity that comes through the shelter of the leaves drops back down into the earth. The wine is absolutely superb, I have to say.

above Painted chapel on Santorini – typical of the architecture on the island.

But what of the food? I hear you cry. Well, by day this charming, picturesque, ancient village is quite simply a shopping mall selling gold, diamonds, coral, designer clothes, electrical goods and expensive, unimaginative paintings. By night it's a disco, selling really bad fast food. It is an immensely popular holiday destination and I was 'Santorini-d out' in something under 18 hours!

From Santorini back to the dreaded Athens for a couple of days, where I cooked in an utterly charming taverna I had now discovered in the Plaka called ΤΑΒΕΡΝΑ ΤΑ ΙΟΥΒΕΤΣΑΚΙΑ. Wonderful souvlakia, moussaka, and chicken with lemon sauce. I cooked a huge bream and took the lemon sauce a stage further by flavouring it with mint and dill, which made it even better than the Greeks can make it.

left Me and the boss.

27

Meteora, Tuesday

From Athens we took a marvellous mountainous route down to the south, some three hours away via Corinth and the Corinth canal – just to look at it, you understand. I couldn't resist being a tourist there! Down to a scruffy little town called Kranidi and then the pretty natural harbour of Portokheli. From thence by hydrofoil – wonderful machine – for a quick obligatory spin around the charming island of Spetses. From there we drove, using ferries, on another equally beautiful journey for 12 hours to Meteora.

above A Kranidi church.

I have travelled to some of the most amazing and wonderful places in the world – to Victoria Falls, the rainforests of Madagascar, the outback of Australia. I have seen poppy farmers in Thailand have their fields blown up by anti-heroin law enforcement agencies; I've flown over the Grand Canyon; I've eaten in the best restaurants in New York and Paris. But I can honestly say that nothing has really gobsmacked me. I suppose this is because television has the effect of lessening our expectations. Even on first sight of the Grand Canyon, marvellous as it is, you just say, 'Yes, that's the Grand Canyon', because you know what to expect.

Driving up to Meteora, on a cool, windy but sunny April day, surrounded by snow-covered mountains, we were confronted with the most incredible rock formations – columns if you like – ledges with sheer sides, reaching up into the sky. Many years ago this was deemed to be a very religious place, and monks built their monasteries on top of these incredibly high columns.

left Portokheli.

There used to be about 25 monasteries in total, like little self-contained villages perched on high, but only about five are still functioning. What is so utterly incredible is that even before they could begin building they had to get everything up there by means of pulleys and ropes – an amazing feat in itself. Every single last thing had to be pulled up these sheer rock faces. And this really did gobsmack me. Looking over at them from a neighbouring ledge at eye level, I couldn't help wondering how on earth the roofer got down when he'd finished. I suffer terribly from vertigo so I stood many, many yards back from the edge whilst filming.

It was in the 11th century that the first hermits took refuge in the caves of Meteora. They found the solitude and the views entirely suitable for their mystic way of life. But when the Serbs invaded (sounds familiar) around the 14th century the monks began to build their monasteries so they could meditate and pray in a paradise somewhere between heaven and earth.

Cynical, jaded traveller I may be, but I would say that if you haven't been to Meteora and you find yourself in Greece, it is truly worth the journey. And the ugly little town of Kalambaka, despite its regular invasions of coaches stuffed with pilgrims, is a lively, friendly place that seems to have more of Greece about it than Athens. In all, a jolly good trip!

P.S. Oh, and by the way, we stopped for food in a filling station dangerously close to the precipitous edge of a mountain pass. A woman was shifting earth in a yellow JCB and a lorry tipped it into the ravine. Inside, two young men were watching weight-lifting on television. I asked if we could eat. 'Just a moment,' he said, and ambled to the door where he shouted to the woman in the JCB. She killed the engine, dusted off her hands, walked in, put on an apron and served us a superbly spicy white bean and vegetable soup, followed by tender rich beef *stifado* (stew) in a thick sauce accompanied by stir-fried dandelions. That simple meal was more heavenly then earthly (and it cost about £4 for three of us).

above Meteora.

29

octopus

A great sight in tatty, whitewashed Greek fishing villages (and in fact throughout the Mediterranean) is octopus hanging under the awnings of al fresco tavernas, spread out like much-washed, ragged laundry. A great smell comes wafting from a rickety, galvanized charcoal barbecue, as pieces of octopus sizzle above a small mound of greying charcoal dust.

In the scruffy port of Kranidi I had a superb breakfast, just as the sun rose, of bread still warm from the baker's oven, grilled octopus with a drop of olive oil, lemon juice and salt, and a glass of ouzo, before embarking upon a fruitless fishing trip where we hauled 19 nets, several kilometres in length, that did not yield one bucket of fish between them. But heck, breakfast was good and so was the ouzo.

Whether you are going to eat octopus cold in a salad, barbecued over charcoal or stewed in a sauce, the first thing you must do is this. Make sure the octopus has been cleaned, cut off the spindly ends of the tentacles and cut all the rest into uniformly bite-sized pieces. Put them into a pan with no liquid whatsoever and cook the octopus in its own juices for about 45 minutes or until they have been reabsorbed. Leave to cool.

Now you can proceed in three different directions. You could thread the octopus on to skewers with little pieces of onion or peppers or both, brush them with olive oil and cook over a charcoal fire – i.e. barbecue them – or you could just marinate the cold cooked pieces in lemon juice and olive oil, season with salt and pepper and add some chopped parsley and coriander. You could add some chopped onion and chopped cold boiled potato to this and make a super little salad if you wanted to. Or you could make the rather smashing dish opposite, ragout of octopus with onions and tomatoes.

ragout of octopus
with onions and tomatoes

2kg/4½lb	octopus, prepared and cooked as described opposite
1.5kg/3¼lb	baby onions of uniform size (about the same size as olives), peeled
	olive oil
6	fat cloves of garlic, finely chopped
About 500ml/ 18fl oz	tomato passata
1 level tbsp	coarsely crushed black peppercorns
2	bay leaves
1	glass of red wine
1	glass of red wine vinegar
	chopped fresh parsley or coriander
	sea salt and black pepper

Fry the octopus and onions in olive oil until the onions are golden, then add the garlic. Add enough tomato sauce almost to cover the onions and octopus, then add the peppercorns, bay leaves, wine, vinegar and salt and simmer gently for about 1 hour, until the octopus is tender and the sauce has reduced. Stick your finger in, lick it and see if you like the sauce. If necessary, add a little more vinegar or salt and pepper. The sauce should be quite thick, tangy and sticking to the octopus rather than the octopus swimming in it.

Sprinkle with parsley or coriander and serve with simple rice.

beef with green olives

Greek stews, or *stifados*, tend to be served quite dry with a highly reduced sauce or gravy. This imparts a huge amount of flavour to the meat and also brings out the full flavour of the sauce. The following ingredients will be enough for roughly 6–8 people, more if you decide to serve it with rice or with macaroni or other pasta (I don't think potatoes are appropriate here).

SERVES 6 - 8

	olive oil
1.5kg/3¼lb	good-quality stewing beef, cut into pieces at least the size of a matchbox
2	large onions, very finely diced
1kg/2¼lb	tomatoes, skinned, deseeded and finely diced (you will end up with about 500g/1lb 2oz diced tomato)
½ bottle	red wine
750g/1lb 10oz	green olives – absolutely NOT tinned ones; use the nice, big, nutty olives (if you wish you can stone them or the guests can spit out the stones)
	sea salt and black pepper

Heat plenty of olive oil in a substantial casserole dish that is large enough to hold the meat in a single layer. Add the beef and fry until it is nicely browned. Now stir in the onions and brown them too. Season with salt and pepper. Next, stir in the tomato dice. Make sure everything is coated with olive oil; if necessary add more. Your pot at this stage should be sizzling, not steaming. Now pour in the red wine, bring to the boil and simmer for about 10 minutes. Stir in the green olives so that all the ingredients are combined, then pop on the lid and cook gently until the meat is tender and the wine and tomatoes have turned themselves into a thick sauce. Check halfway through the cooking process. If it is looking too dry, add a little more wine.

grilled fish with lemon sauce

This dish is ideal for those of you fortunate enough to have either a *plancha* (a large cast-iron plate heated by gas) or a genuine charcoal barbecue. On a fine day you can cook the fish outside and prepare the sauce in the kitchen at the same time.

I used a black bream weighing about 2.25kg/5lb but you could use any fish – big or small, it doesn't matter. Ask the fishmonger to gut the fish and trim off all the fins but leave the scales on as these will burn away during cooking. Stuff the fish with some chopped parsley, wedges of lemon, celery leaves, salt and pepper. Rub the fish well with salt and olive oil and whack it on a severely hot *plancha* or barbecue.

Meanwhile, prepare your sauce. You will need 25g/1oz butter and 2 tablespoons flour, about 300ml/½ pint lemon juice, 4 egg yolks beaten together with 2 whole eggs, plus some chopped fresh mint and dill.

Melt the butter in a pan, stir in the flour and cook until smooth. Now whisk in the lemon juice and cook, stirring all the time, until you have a smooth liquid. Pull away from the heat and, while whisking furiously, slowly pour in the beaten eggs. Keep whisking off the heat until the sauce thickens to the consistency of hollandaise or runny mayonnaise. Taste it and see if you need to add any salt and pepper, then stir in mint and dill to taste. The sauce is then simply poured over the cooked fish. It is very popular in Greece and can be served with virtually anything that is edible, even, strangely enough, luscious ripe strawberries that have already been marinated without sugar in lemon juice. I'm not joking – try it! A splendid accompaniment to this dish is the pasta rice with spinach below.

pasta rice
with spinach

1 packet	orzo (pasta shaped like grains of rice)
	olive oil
6	spring onions, chopped into 2.5cm/ 1 inch batons, both green and white parts
2	garlic cloves, chopped
1	large bunch of fresh spinach, chopped
a pinch	of cinnamon
1 cup	blanched almonds, pine nuts or walnuts – any kind of nut that takes your fancy
1 cup	raisins
	sea salt and black pepper

Cook the pasta in plenty of boiling salted water until *al dente*, then drain. Pour in a little olive oil to stop the grains sticking together and keep warm.

While the pasta is cooking, fry the spring onions and garlic in olive oil for a few minutes, then add the chopped spinach and stir-fry until wilted, mixing it with the onions and garlic. Season with salt and pepper and a pinch of cinnamon. Meanwhile, in a hot dry frying pan toast the nuts and raisins.

To serve, simply stir the spinach mixture and the toasted nuts and raisins into the pasta.

Toujours le garlic

In common with that of other countries along the Mediterranean coastline, the traditional cooking of the South of France was based on indigenous local produce and what could be fished from the sea. In the days before motorized transport and refrigeration, cooks along the coast would fill their larders with ingredients from probably no more than a 50-mile radius of their homes. Thus the essential elements of Mediterranean cookery were proscribed by climate and terrain, which is both harsh and beautiful, and only occasionally soft.

Inland from the coast, on the arid hills where only gorse, broom, olive trees, thyme, lavender, rosemary and wild fennel can survive, there was no suitable grazing for cows but goats and sheep thrived. As a consequence there was no butter and no cow's milk cheese. Instead soft, fresh, creamy cheeses were made from goat's and sheep's milk during the milking season. For winter they were either dried until they became hard, crunchy, chalky bricks, or *banons*, or they were preserved in olive oil.

The scrub-covered hills, the *maquis* (the French Resistance was known as the Maquis because it was able to hide well in the scrub), provide a superb habitat for rabbits, hares and all manner of birds. In the same way that lamb grazed on wild herbs tastes so good, honey gathered from bees that have danced over lavender tastes fine and exotic. On the slopes of fertile valleys, cherries, apricots, almonds and vines thrive under the Mediterranean sun. Melons, aubergines, peppers, courgettes, tomatoes and garlic grow abundantly.

aubergine caviar on toast

As I mentioned in the Greek section of this book, the aubergine is one of the most versatile vegetables in the Mediterranean. So here's another way to enjoy it, as what the French call an *amuse-bouche*, the Greeks *mezze*, the Spanish *tapas*, and some people use that dreadful expression 'finger food'.

About 675g/ **1½lb**	aubergines
1	small tin of anchovy fillets in olive oil, drained
1 tbsp	tapenade, which is basically black olives, garlic, capers, lemon juice and olive oil whizzed to a purée in a food processor, or, of course, you can buy it ready made
	olive oil
	red or white wine vinegar
1	baguette, cut into slices 5mm/¼ inch thick
	sea salt and black pepper

Roast the aubergines as for stuffed vegetables (see page 49) and leave to cool. Scrape out the pulp and put it in a food processor with the anchovy fillets, tapenade, a dash of olive oil and a drop or two of wine vinegar. Process to a purée, then season with sea salt and black pepper.

Brush the baguette slices with olive oil on both sides and toast quickly in a dry frying pan. Spread the aubergine caviar on to the toasts and that's it.

below The harbour at Cannes.

fish soup

As well as the ubiquitous *assiette de fruits de mer*, every restaurant along the French Mediterranean coast serves fish soup – very often from a tin or bottle which, ironically, in some cases is really rather better than the homemade version served in those erratic port-side restaurants. The real secret to making a good fish soup is being able to acquire what is known as *poissons de roche*. This is a colourful selection of small fish netted ruthlessly but necessarily and specifically for this dish. You will often see them advertised in French markets as *soupe de poisson*. So you need about a kilo of this. If you can't buy it, you can use such things as small gurnard, red mullet, soft-shelled crabs, red snapper, etc. All need to be gutted, scaled and de-finned, then chopped into fairly small pieces.

4	garlic cloves, very finely chopped
1	large carrot, finely diced
1	leek, with green part, chopped
1 large	stick of celery with its leaves, chopped
4 large	ripe tomatoes, roughly chopped
1	onion, finely diced
	chopped fresh fennel fronds or 1 small fennel bulb, finely diced
	olive oil
1kg/2¼lb	mixed fish (see opposite)
a large pinch	of saffron strands
	sea salt and black pepper

FOR THE AÏOLI:

10	garlic cloves, peeled
2	egg yolks
1	egg
about 300ml/ ½ pint	olive oil
	lemon juice
TO SERVE:	thin rounds of baguette, fried on both sides in olive oil
	finely grated Parmesan cheese (optional)

First make the aïoli: purée the garlic in a food processor, then add the egg yolks and whole egg and process until well amalgamated. With the motor still running, slowly pour in enough olive oil to make a thick mayonnaise. Season with lemon juice, salt and pepper.

Fry the garlic, carrot, leek, celery, tomatoes, onion and fennel in olive oil until soft. Add the fish and about 1.7 litres/3 pints of water, bring quickly to the boil, then turn down to a simmer. Once the fish is cooked, ladle the fish and liquid into a food processor and blend. Then strain it through a fine sieve into another saucepan, pushing it through the sieve with a spoon so that all the fleshy bits go through but not the bones and things. Reheat the soup very gently, add the saffron, season with sea salt and black pepper and that's it. To serve, spread the warm croûtons of French bread with aïoli and float them in the individual bowls of soup. The grated cheese is an optional extra for people to sprinkle on to their soup.

Provençal omelette cake

The idea of this dish is to make several thin omelettes, each one flavoured differently, then stack them on top of each other to make a cake, weight it down, and cut into small wedges to nibble with your apéritif.

2	large tomatoes, skinned, deseeded and finely diced
	olive oil
2	decent-sized garlic cloves, finely chopped
1	large courgette, partly peeled, then deseeded and finely chopped
2	shallots, finely diced
8–10	eggs
2 heaped tbsp	freshly grated Parmesan cheese
½ cup	finely chopped cooked spinach
1	large red pepper, roasted, skinned and finely chopped
	butter
	sea salt and black pepper

Fry the tomatoes briefly in olive oil with half the garlic and some salt and pepper, then transfer to a plate to cool. Fry the courgette with the remaining garlic in the same way, then place on a separate plate to cool. Fry the shallots in a little olive oil, then season and set aside.

Next whisk the eggs with a little salt and pepper and a dash of water until frothy and divide between 5 small bowls, or as many bowls as you wish to make omelettes. If you don't have 5 small bowls, use teacups. Then simply put your tomato mixture into one lot of egg, courgette in the next, Parmesan cheese and shallots in the next, spinach in the next, red pepper in the next. Mix each one up, then heat a drop of butter and a dash of olive oil in a small omelette pan and set about making the omelettes. Place the first cooked one on a plate, then make the next one and stack it on top of the first. Keep making and stacking until you have a multi-layered omelette cake. Put a plate and a large can of baked beans or something similar on top and leave to cool, then put it in the fridge. Cut into small wedges to serve.

From this rich but simple larder, influenced by spices, dried fruit and nuts introduced from Africa, the stunning simplicity of sun cooking evolved. Powerful fish soups flavoured with saffron, crude to those who exalted the creamy bisques of the lactose north. A melange of aubergines, courgettes, peppers and tomatoes, stewed simply in olive oil to make ratatouille. A stoned apricot filled with fresh goat's cheese. Lamb perfumed with fragrant, sundried herbs, grilled over a fire of vine roots. Salted cod served with simply cooked vegetables and a mountain of aïoli. Sweet salads of sun-ripened tomatoes and olives. Huge plates of fresh shellfish grilled with garlic, parsley and olive oil. Country bread spread with tapenade, a purée of black olives. The simple vegetable soup – a French minestrone if you like – called *soupe au pistou*, *pistou* being a Provençal word for a type of pesto made with basil, pine nuts and olive oil. Just before the soup is served, a

large dollop of *pistou* is thrown in. Thick yellow omelettes stuffed with truffles, almost like a Spanish tortilla, eaten cold by country folk for their working lunch. Sea bass grilled over charcoal and, then, at the last minute flamed over a faggot of dried fennel twigs. Pastis and coarse red wines. In winter time, slow-simmered stews of rabbit or hare. The list is endless. To paraphrase Ford Maddox Ford: 'South of Lyons the apple cannot survive and the Brussels sprout cannot grow.' The point being that once you pass that imaginary line and see the olive trees you know you are in a different gastronomic world.

But today there is a rapid transport system, refrigeration and all the trappings of modern life, and regional distinctions have become irrevocably blurred. The Mediterranean coast can no longer boast its fierce independence. Depressingly, the seaside towns and ports seem to be a parody of something that was once passionate and individual. The great Mediterranean dishes – the aïoli, the *soupe de poisson*, the *assiette de fruits de mer*, the bouillabaisse, the bourride, the paellas and the risottos, the *friture de poisson* – have often been debased through commercial expediency or callousness and have become insipid imitations. To make matters worse, the so-called specialist restaurants, with their mountains of oysters, mussels and clams and their refrigerated displays of bass, mullet and octopus, John Dory and bream, monkfish and all, jostle side by side with deep-pan pizza shops, Planet Hollywood and McDonalds.

But the French cling to their gastronomic illusions and, at the first sign of summer, they stampede from the cities to the coast to indulge their passion for fish and seafood. On a Sunday at about midday I wandered past eight or ten restaurants with their tiny tables squeezed closely together on the pavement under bright awnings. Each one was full. The customers sat in their Sunday best, morosely munching from identical platters of *fruits de mer* before attacking the speciality of aïoli or grilled fish or whatever – not necessarily because it was good but because that's what you do when you come to the coast. I felt sorry for them all and smugly continued up the road to the Vesuvius restaurant, where I had a salad of frisée, lardons, crunchy croûtons, olive oil and a poached egg, then a thin, crisp pizza with a rich tomato base, cheese and anchovies, which I seasoned with a few drops of herb and chilli olive oil, followed by creamy goat's cheese and a bowl of cherries. That simple meal had more fun, more sun, more of the Mediterranean than a thousand *assiettes de fruits de mer*.

left Seafood passion in Cannes.

POSTCARDS
FROM FRANCE

Cannes,
Wednesday

Cannes is packed with people. The streets are barricaded and the Cannes Film Festival one-way traffic system is creating honking, raging havoc as I glide down the boulevard in the back of a grotesque replica of a Thirties' American sports car, driven by a tall, thin, shaven-headed, black-suited chauffeur who looks like a minor baddy from a Bond film. The people, pressing against the barriers, wave and take pictures as we sweep into the Carlton Hotel, clearly thinking that I must be some kind of movie star. Because our camera crew is filming my arrival, other crews think I am important and start shooting too. I pull down the brim of my hat and dash for the door. My 15 seconds of glory! I understand enough French to hear people say, 'Who was that?' The foyer is packed with journalists, cameramen, PR people and security men, all clutching glossy brochures and wearing laminated identification tags. Everybody is talking into a mobile phone. Porters are dragging trolleys piled high with Louis Vuitton cases through the mêlée. Four drinks in the bar cost £38!

It is a fine evening so we stroll down to the old port. All the restaurants and cafés are full and there is a great carnival atmosphere. Photographers and camera crews cruise the strip looking for celebrities. As we sit at a restaurant table with the sinking realization that we've picked a bummer, I order *gratin de moules à la Provençale* and get served six still partially frozen New Zealand green-lipped mussels with a bit of chopped parsley thrown over. We decide to grin and bear it, and end up paying £70 for our stupidity.

left I felt really embarrassed riding in this awful car.

gratin of mussels and spinach

SERVES 4 – 6

1.5kg/3¼lb	fresh mussels
1	generous glass of dry white wine
25g/1oz	butter
2 tbsp	plain flour
	milk
150ml/¼ pint	double cream or crème fraîche
a pinch	freshly grated nutmeg
4 cups	finely chopped cooked fresh spinach (stir-fry the leaves without their stalks in just a tiny bit of butter – do not use water)
4 tbsp	grated hard cheese
	black pepper

Scrub and debeard the mussels and, with your thumb and forefinger, try to open the shell of each one. If it doesn't open that's perfect. If it does open you will find it is full of very, very fine sand which will completely ruin the dish, so you must check each mussel and throw away any open ones. Put the mussels into a large pan, add the white wine (no other liquid), cover with a tight-fitting lid and cook the mussels over a medium heat until the shells have opened. Strain the mussels and reserve the resulting juices. Remove the mussels from their shells, discarding any that haven't opened, and put to one side. Melt the butter in a pan, stir in the flour and cook for a moment or two to make a roux. Make the reserved mussel-cooking juices up to 300ml/½ pint with milk if necessary and whisk them into the roux. Bring to the boil, whisking, until you have a smooth sauce. Finish it off by stirring in the cream. Season with grated nutmeg and black pepper.

Mix the spinach and mussels together in a shallow gratin dish. Pour over the white sauce, sprinkle the cheese over the top and grill until golden brown.

45

Thursday

Aborted journey to Fréjus to visit Roman ruins. A complete waste of time. A hastily contrived plan B finds us at Cannes market just behind the *hôtel de ville* by the old port.

In Greece I had problems shopping for food and even in France it can sometimes be difficult. Not so here. Cannes market, small though it is, is one of the best I have ever been to. Not only is the produce plentiful, varied, fresh and local but the stallholders – maybe a little old lady selling bunches of dried thyme, rosemary and fennel, or an elegant woman behind the fresh pasta stall with perfectly manicured fingernails and swept-up blond hair tied in a pony tail, or the ruddy-faced fishermen standing behind piles of still-flapping fish – are universally cheerful and obliging, and join in with our filming with great relish. Even the lady at the wild mushroom stall, who scolds me for handling her delicate produce, gives me a couple of extra grams for free, and I promise her I will never do it again!

A simple sequence where we are walking down the street pausing at a shellfish stall to explain the importance of the *assiette de fruits de mer* becomes a nightmare. Usually I can do my pieces to camera in one, maybe two, takes. This one goes to 14. Every time I arrive at the stall I simply have to say, 'Fresh oysters, mussels, crabs, prawns, clams, whelks and shrimps.' Thirteen times in succession I get there and cannot remember the names of any of the things on the stall.

I spend the rest of the afternoon doing driving shots in the absurd white automobile along the precipitous but beautiful Cannes coast road, where, on a cliff, Yves St Laurent built a house that looks like a space station made of glass igloos. That evening, about 200 yards behind Planet Hollywood, we find a brilliant self-service Asian restaurant run by Vietnamese and have an excellent meal with wine for £14 for two.

Friday

Day devoted to gambling and cooking – at least that's what it will look like in the programme! The people at the Carlton Casino are really helpful and, by the magic of television, I in my dinner jacket win thousands and thousands playing roulette, only to lose the lot on the last throw of the evening which, by the predictability of clichéed television, finds me back in the kitchen cooking my stuffed vegetables and red mullet with tomatoes and olives in the middle of 19 chefs who are preparing frantically for that evening's two-star Michelin dinner. They need us like a hole in the head, with our lights and monitors and cables. To make matters worse, the air conditioning breaks down and by some bizarre freak the drains go into reverse and the kitchen floor is flooded. Kim Sayer, our stills photographer, wants to shoot my finished dishes on the balcony of the restaurant. While he is setting up, a seagull swoops down and swipes the mullet off the plate. All in all, just another shitty day in paradise!

above Just before the fall.

sauté of new potatoes
with wild mushrooms and glazed onions

approx 900g/2lb	small, uniformly sized, scrubbed new potatoes
	olive oil or goose fat
750g/1½lb	wild mushrooms, e.g. girolles or morelles, or, at a pinch, little white button mushrooms
	butter
1	shallot, finely chopped
1	sprig of thyme
225g/8oz	baby onions, peeled
1 tbsp	sugar
	sea salt and black pepper

First sauté the potatoes gently in olive oil or goose fat until they are cooked and golden.

In another pan, sauté the mushrooms in butter with the chopped shallot, the fresh thyme and some sea salt and pepper. In another pan, just cover the onions with water and add a knob of butter and the sugar. Bring to the boil and then simmer gently for about 15 minutes or until the onions are cooked and the water has evaporated, leaving the onions lightly browned and glazed. Combine all the ingredients in a serving dish and serve with something like a simply grilled veal chop, which is exactly what I did at the two-star Michelin restaurant attached to the Carlton Casino in Cannes for the chef, Francis Chauveau.

right The wonderful
food market in Cannes.

red mullet
with tomatoes and olives

Red mullet is not compulsory. Grey mullet will do, as will John Dory, bass or bream.

SERVES 4

6	sticks of dried fennel
4	tomatoes, roughly chopped
2	lemons, sliced into very thin rounds
4	plump red mullet, gutted, scaled and fins removed
2 cups	chicken stock or dry white wine
	olive oil
	butter
about 20	black olives, stoned
about 2 tbsp	chopped fresh basil
	sea salt and black pepper

First lay the fennel sticks in a baking tray. Spread the tomatoes and half the lemon slices over them. Then place the red mullet on top and pour over the chicken stock or wine. Cover the fish with the remaining lemon slices. Shake in a few drops of olive oil, season with salt and pepper and bake in an oven preheated to 200°C/400°F/Gas Mark 6 for 10–15 minutes, until the fish is just cooked, not overcooked.

Transfer the fish to a serving dish and keep warm. Strain the liquid from the baking tray into a saucepan, bring to the boil and boil until reduced by about two thirds. Over a low heat, whisk in several knobs of butter until you have a smooth sauce. Then whisk in a drop of olive oil, which will not combine with the butter sauce but will form little glistening droplets on the surface. Add the stoned black olives to warm them through. Meanwhile, quickly fillet the fish. Pour over the sauce and sprinkle on the chopped basil.

stuffed vegetables

100g/4oz	sundried tomatoes, coarsely chopped
	olive oil
2	boneless, skinless chicken breasts, cut in half lengthways
4	slices of boneless lamb (same weight as the chicken)
4–5	shallots, finely chopped
2–3	garlic cloves, finely chopped
	butter
100g/4oz	white mushrooms, finely chopped
1 cup	finely chopped fresh parsley
generous ½ cup	freshly grated Parmesan cheese
4	aubergines, as near round as possible
4	round courgettes, if possible, or the bottom half of 4 large courgettes
4 large	round tomatoes
½ cup	chicken or veal stock
	juice of 2 lemons
	sea salt and black pepper

Gently sauté the sundried tomatoes in olive oil for about 15 minutes, then set aside to cool in their oil.

Heat a little olive oil in a heavy-based pan until very hot and sear the chicken breasts and lamb on both sides until they are nicely chargrilled. The meat must be raw in the middle because it is going to be cooked again and will be too dry if overcooked at this stage. Leave the meat to cool, then, using a large knife and not a food processor, chop very finely. Put into a large mixing bowl and set aside. Next fry the shallots and garlic in butter until golden, then add the finely

chopped mushrooms and cook until tender. Stir this mixture into the chopped meat. Add the parsley and Parmesan cheese and mix together. Season to taste.

Rub the aubergines with a little oil, salt and pepper, then roast in an oven preheated to its highest temperature for about 20 minutes or until tender. Leave to cool. Meanwhile, blanch the courgettes in lightly salted boiling water for about 5 minutes, then drain well and leave to cool. Cut the top off the tomatoes and scoop out and discard the flesh and pips. Now divide the meat and mushroom mixture into three. Cut the top off the aubergines, scrape out the pulp and mix with the first portion of stuffing. Ditto for the courgettes. But for the tomatoes you add the chopped sundried tomatoes to their separate pile of stuffing. Stuff the vegetables with their appropriate mixtures, place in a well-oiled baking tray and season with salt and pepper. Add the stock and lemon juice and a few knobs of butter and bake in an oven preheated to 200°C/400°F/Gas Mark 6 for 20 or 30 minutes, until the vegetables are nicely browned. They can be eaten hot with the juices from the baking tray or served cold with a lemon and olive oil vinaigrette.

Hôtel de Paris, Monaco, Saturday

As you can see from the postcard, I am staying in unadulterated luxury. The restaurant is sensational and its chef, Alain Ducasse, is, I believe, the only man in France to have two three-starred restaurants. Earlier I spent a few hours with the racing driver Johnny Herbert, who drove me around the Grand Prix circuit in his convertible BMW, during which time we were briefly arrested for apparently filming without permission. A few phone calls solved that quite quickly. Managed to get invited aboard a huge 300-foot yacht for drinks and exquisite canapés. I think the only notable absentee was Nigel Dempster ... but there was another, bigger boat in the harbour. Oh and by the way, in case you can't afford the Hôtel de Paris, try the Café de Paris opposite. It certainly restored my flagging faith in ordinary French cooking.

Cannes, Monday

Take the ferry to the island of Saint Honorat, a journey of about 30 or 40 minutes. It reminds me very much of Tresco in the Scilly Isles. It has had a monastery since the 5th century and recently the monks have replanted vines. They make a red wine that tastes strongly of the island itself – fresh salt air and resinous pines – quite unusual but

above Nigel Hawthorne, and ...

pleasantly distinctive. I ask the good brother how they market their wine and he says, 'All of it, all over the world, on the Internet.' He smiles.

The afternoon tranquillity is shattered by the arrival of a couple of unruly crocodiles of Italian schoolchildren, screaming and yelling.

Return to the mainland and have a couple of drinks with Sir Nigel Hawthorne, who is here to promote four films in which he is appearing. Tomorrow we are flying home via Madrid to unpack and re-pack and head off for Cairo.

blanquette of vegetables

About 600ml/	
1 pint	chicken or veal stock
8	baby carrots, scraped
4 small	turnips, peeled and cut in half
6–8 small	white onions (spring onions if possible)
3 large	courgettes, halved, deseeded and quartered
225g/8oz	white button mushrooms
225g/8oz	wild mushrooms (e.g. ceps or chanterelles), if available
150 ml/¼ pint	double cream
50g/2oz	unsalted butter
	lemon juice
225g/8oz	fresh spinach leaves, stalks removed, leaves roughly chopped
	sea salt

This fresh and fragrant dish of vegetables goes equally well with fish, meat or chicken. I served it to the racing driver Johnny Herbert just before the Monaco Grand Prix, with simple brochettes of rabbit which I had marinated in lemon juice, olive oil, garlic and fresh thyme. Although Johnny finished thirteenth in the race he didn't blame my cooking for his disappointment!

Bring the stock to the boil and, starting with the carrots, cook each type of vegetable (but not the spinach) separately in the stock, removing them as they are done before adding the next lot. Put the vegetables on a serving platter and keep warm. Now boil the stock until it is reduced to about half to three-quarters of a cupful. Whisk in the cream, then whisk in little knobs of the butter until the sauce is thick. Season with lemon juice to taste. Add the roughly chopped spinach and heat through for just 1 minute, then pour the sauce over the vegetables. Sprinkle on some coarse sea salt.

... Johnny Herbert.

Turkish delight?

Turkish cooking is similar to that of Greece but a little more sophisticated, and frequently a little spicier, especially when flaked chillies and cumin are used. The Turks have a fondness for adding nuts and dried fruit to savoury dishes and, like the Greeks, use a lot of yoghurt and lemon. Also, both Greeks and Turks eat mezzes. But, as is common the world over these days, it is easier to find the fragrant and exotic dishes of Turkey within the lavishly illustrated pages of cookery books than it is in indigenous restaurants.

On Sunday, the Galata Bridge in Istanbul is crawling with people desperate for a breath of fresh air on a hot July afternoon. Hawkers flog cheap watches, old shoes, bankrupt electronics and garish piles of meaningless tat. Fishermen, in a triumph of hope over experience, catch small fish on their long rods and a boy with a small barbecue will cook it for you. The leaden, swirling Bosphorus is crisscrossed furiously by packed maroon and green ferries, snapping fearlessly, like water terriers, at the heels of the burnt-sienna rusted hulks of overladen, ore-carrying Russian tankers, which grind through the straits to the Black Sea, T-shirts and jeans hanging to dry from a rusty porthole. The gantries and cranes of these wrecks reflect sinisterly, like black gibbets in the dying ochre sun.

above The Old Summer Palace, Istanbul.

far left River traffic on the Bosphorus.

55

stuffed fish baked
in filo pastry

SERVES 4

4 tbsp coarsely crushed pistachio nuts (shelled, of course)

4 tbsp sultanas or currants

4 thick fillets of fish, such as sea bass, salmon or bream, skinned

4 very thin slices of lemon

8 fresh mint leaves

2 knobs of butter

8 sheets of filo pastry

½ cup melted butter

sea salt and black pepper

FOR THE SAUCE:

a knob of butter

1 heaped tbsp flour

2 wineglasses fresh lemon juice

3 egg yolks, beaten

½ cup chopped fresh mint or dried mint

Mix the nuts and sultanas or currants together and spread the whole amount over 2 of the fish fillets. Put the lemon slices on top and then put the mint leaves on top of the lemon. Season with salt and pepper. Put a knob of butter in the centre of each fillet, then place the 2 remaining fillets on top.

Paint a sheet of filo pastry with melted butter and place one of the stuffed fish fillets on it. Wrap it neatly in a parcel, trimming off any excess pastry. Repeat this process until you have used up 4 sheets of pastry per fish. Paint again lightly with butter, place the parcels on a baking sheet and pop into a very hot oven for 12–15 minutes. When the pastry is golden brown, push a skewer into the centre of the fish and leave it for a moment or two; if it comes out hot, the fish is cooked.

For the sauce, melt the butter in a pan and stir in the flour to make a roux. Cook, stirring, for a minute or two, then gradually whisk in the lemon juice until you have a smooth sauce. Over a low heat, whisk the egg yolks rapidly into the sauce until it thickens, then stir in the mint. Taste and add a little salt and pepper if necessary.

To serve, divide the sauce between 4 plates, cut the fish parcels in half and place on top of the sauce.

right The results of overfishing –

empty stalls and undersized fish.

left The Blue
Mosque, Istanbul.

right Entrance to
the Blue Mosque.

My taxi is clean, polished and old. I cannot wind down the rear window because vandals have taken the handles, and there is no air conditioning. Over the bridge, we turn left past the spice bazaar, past the bus station and the ferry port, and grind up the hill towards the Blue Mosque, which looks as if it has been made in concrete and shipped from Didcot power station. Let me tell you, although it is an outstanding piece of architecture and – given that it was constructed in the 14th–16th centuries – a considerable piece of engineering, it is not blue!

As we climb the hill, the streets empty and the traffic lights are perverse. We pull into a narrower street with drab, three-storey buildings containing shops selling generators, dynamos, guns, rubber tubing and galvanized containers. Laundry is drying from the windows above. There is the occasional shop window filled with orthopaedic goods, or a spectacles shop, or a pharmacist with a dusty display of health foods and patent medicines. We are not far from the Grand Bazaar, a rabbit warren of vaulted arcades where leather, gold, tapestry and embroidery are touted to screaming point by handsome Turks who can give you the best price and have also been to Brighton. 'Do you come from Brighton?' they ask

right Doesn't
look blue inside!

and if you don't, don't say, 'I come from Nottingham,' because they will have been there too. But on Sunday the Grand Bazaar is closed and the generator shops have no clients and only the odd cat patrols the streets. There is an archway between an audio shop and a barber's. Take six steps down, open the mahogany door and step into what looks like a cross between a panelled Victorian station ticket office and a 1912 New Orleans brothel. In this semi-circular foyer, either side of a heavy planked door, are two staircases that spiral to galleried private salons. In front of the heavy door is a polished hardwood desk, and in front of this a trestle table piled high with folded towels. Behind the desk sit swarthy men, glistening with oil and wrapped in towels. They have tattoos, they are not curious as anyone enters, they are smoking and trimming each other's moustache with a pair of scissors. I am offered a glass of hot, sweet tea and shown to a

left The fish market
on the Galata bridge.

cubicle, where I am given slippers, trunks and a towel. A giant
of a man, who says his name is Vulcan, takes me through the
heavy door into the inner sanctum. It is a circular room with a
domed ceiling and open skylights. In the centre is a marble disc,
two feet off the floor and about seven yards in diameter. There
are tiled troughs of water around the perimeter of the room and
heavy, tarnished brass taps. Some men are lying on this marble
plancha like fat tuna fish, wrapped in towels and being soaked,
pummelled and hosed down. I am lying on my back looking at
the skylights as Vulcan pummels my muscles, or what I
laughingly call my muscles. Every now and again he throws a

bucket of tepid water over me and then bends another limb beyond any reasonable geometric position. After pulling my fingers off my hand and splitting my toes in half he douses me with buckets of ice-cold water. Before I know what is happening, his massive hands are on the back of my neck, forcing it between my knees. He then scrubs my head with shampoo and pushes me back on to the marble to rest.

It is at this moment, as I drift away into semi-consciousness, that I begin to wonder about Istanbul, the only city that is built on two continents, Europe and Asia, in a country that is lapped by the Mediterranean, the Marmara, the Bosphorus and the Black Sea. Both country and city have played a profound part, not only in gastronomic history but also in world history. Once the capital of the Roman Empire, once, through the Orient Express, the fabled destination of the mysterious rich and famous, such as

below The Mosque of Süleyman.

above 'Fish Street', Istanbul – a favourite eating area.

Greta Garbo, Graham Greene and Sarah Bernhardt. Once the home of spies. A city rich in culture yet devastated by political ineptitude and, from time to time, as I was sad to witness, albeit from a safe distance, destroyed by earthquakes.

As I lay on the slab, I revisited in my mind the Perla Palace, where Agatha Christie wrote *Murder on the Orient Express*. I tasted the mackerel sandwiches you can buy on the busy harbour and the sweet tea from the impossibly heavy urns that they carry on their backs in the bus station. I wondered about the spice market where you can now buy more brass peppermills than you can spices. I wondered about the Ottoman Empire that once stretched from Egypt to Hungary and I wondered why they say that Turkish cuisine stands alongside those of France, China and India.

The reason, I suppose, is that it has developed from the grand kitchens of the Sultans' palaces over about 1,000 years. I doubt that even the Sun King in his palace at Versailles had as many cooks as the Topkapi Palace, where some 1,300 kitchen staff fed as many as 10,000 a day.

right Entrance to the covered bazaar, Istanbul.

left The Dalyan river is

not the cleanest of places!

Floyd's Turkish barbecue

A little note on barbecuing food in the fresh air: there are no weights, measures, cooking times or temperatures in the recipes that follow because, for example, the number of cubes of lamb you put on a skewer would depend on the length of the skewer you are using. The time it takes to cook a minced lamb patty over a charcoal fire will depend upon its size and the heat of the charcoal which, as I have explained elsewhere in this book, is not ready to use until all the flames are extinguished and it is covered in off-white or grey powder. It is at this moment that the charcoal is at its hottest.

After an exhilarating morning whitewater rafting, albeit in a fairly calm Dalyan river, I prepared the following lunch for the exuberant and hungry rafters.

vegetable kebabs

onions
aubergines
tomatoes
peppers
courgettes
olive oil
dried herbs such as thyme and rosemary
sea salt and black pepper

Slice the vegetables into pieces of the same size, except for the tomatoes which should be cut in half. Thread on skewers in a colourful manner and then marinate in olive oil and dried herbs for about an hour. Place on the barbecue and cook, turning occasionally, until tender. Season with salt and pepper.

lamb kebabs

1	leg of lamb, boned
	a sheet of lamb fat or, if unobtainable, pork fat (although this would be unacceptable in Turkey, where the majority of the population is Muslim; if you are a pork eater the pork fat will in no way impair the flavour of the lamb – if anything, it will add to it)
	lemons
	onions
	olive oil
	dried thyme
	sea salt and black pepper

Dice the lamb meat into 4cm/1½ inch cubes. Cut the fat into slices the same height as the cubed lamb. Cut the lemons and onions into segments of the same size. Place on skewers in this order: onion, fat, meat, lemon, onion, fat, meat, lemon. Marinate in olive oil and dried thyme for about an hour. Place on a barbecue and cook, turning, until the meat is sealed on all sides, then season with salt and pepper.

lamb kofte

1kg/2¼lb	minced lamb
	dried mint to taste
	sea salt and black pepper

Mix the lamb and mint together and then make into tablepoon-sized patties. Place on the barbecue and cook until sealed on both sides. Season with salt and pepper.

sauces for barbecues

SAUCE ONE

500ml/18fl oz	best-quality plain yoghurt
1 heaped tbsp	tomato purée
½ tsp	Turkish chilli flakes

Whisk all the ingredients together and chill until required.

SAUCE TWO

1	cucumber, peeled, deseeded and grated
500ml/18fl oz	best-quality plain yoghurt
	a handful of chopped rocket
	chopped fresh dill
	chopped fresh parsley
	sea salt

Put the cucumber in a colander, sprinkle with sea salt and leave to drain for 30 minutes–1 hour (this gets rid of excess moisture). Pat dry on kitchen paper, then mix with all the other ingredients.

a simple salad

equal quantities of cucumber, tomatoes and spring onions
lemon juice
olive oil
peeled garlic cloves
sea salt and black pepper

Peel and deseed the cucumber and chop into 1cm/½ inch cubes. Blanch the tomatoes quickly in boiling water, skin and deseed them, then chop into pieces the same size as the cucumber. Chop the spring onions the same size, too. Mix the lot together with some sea salt and leave in a colander for about an hour to drain. Pat dry on kitchen paper, then place in a salad bowl.

Using a liquidizer, mix to your taste some lemon juice, olive oil, garlic, salt and pepper to make a dressing to pour over the salad. You might like to add some mustard and sugar – try it and see.

quail stuffed with rice, walnuts and sultanas

If you make these first, then prepare the kebabs, everything should be ready at the same time.

FOR EACH PERSON	
6	vine leaves
2	boned quail, with leg bones still attached (ask your butcher to do this)
2 tbsp	Turkish rice (see below)
1 tbsp	chopped walnuts
1 tbsp	sultanas
	sea salt and black pepper

Lay out the vine leaves and place one quail on top, skin-side down. Season with salt and pepper. Put the rice, chopped walnuts and sultanas on top of the quail. Place the other quail on top and wrap in the vine leaves, leaving the legs protruding. Wrap in foil and seal both ends. Place on the barbecue and cook for about 40 minutes, turning the package every 10 minutes.

Turkish rice

1kg/2¼lb	long grain rice
4	onions, finely chopped
6	cloves of garlic, finely chopped
	olive oil
	chicken stock
	cinnamon
	Turkish red chilli flakes

Wash the rice and then drain thoroughly. Fry the onions and garlic in olive oil until tender. Add the rice and fry until translucent. Add enough chicken stock to cover the rice and cook gently with the lid on for 6–8 minutes. Add the cinnamon and chilli flakes to taste and cook for a further 2–3 minutes or until the rice is done. This dish can be eaten hot or cold.

sauté of chicken
with pistachios and orange sauce

SERVES 4

4	boned and skinned chicken breasts
100g/4oz	shelled pistachio nuts, crushed
4	thin slices of cheese, such as Kasar (Turkish ewe's milk cheese) or Gruyère
1	egg, beaten with 1 tablespoon milk
	flour for dusting
	butter
1 glass	of Raki (a Turkish aniseed liquor) or pastis
	juice of 2 oranges
	pithless segments of 2 oranges
	sea salt and black pepper

Put the chicken breasts between 2 sheets of clingfilm and beat gently with a meat mallet or a rolling pin to make thin escalopes. Sprinkle each one with the pistachio nuts and season with salt and pepper. Lay a slice of cheese on top of the nuts, then roll each breast into a cigar shape and secure with a wooden cocktail stick. Dunk the chicken into the beaten egg mixture and then roll it in flour. Shake off excess flour and fry the chicken in butter in a shallow pan until golden all over, turning from time to time. This should take 15–20 minutes. When you think the chicken is cooked, pour in the Raki and flame the chicken – let the Raki heat up for a second or two, then set it alight, standing well back. Whisk it into the butter and juices in the pan.

Remove the chicken and keep warm. Add the orange juice to the pan over a fierce heat and boil until reduced and slightly syrupy. Season to taste, then whisk in a knob of butter to make the sauce smooth and creamy. Strain the sauce into a clean pan, add the orange segments and heat through gently. Then pour the sauce over the chicken and serve.

minced beef and spinach

1	bunch of spring onions
12	small okra, trimmed
2	cloves of garlic, finely chopped
	olive oil
	butter
250g/9oz	minced beef
1 tbsp	paprika
1 tbsp	ground allspice
1 tbsp	dried chilli flakes
1kg/2¼lb	fresh spinach leaves (no stems), coarsely chopped
	sea salt and black pepper
1 tub	plain yoghurt, to serve

First chop the spring onions, both green and white bits, into pieces about 2.5cm/1 inch long. Stir-fry them with the okra, half the garlic and some salt and pepper in olive oil over a high heat for a minute or so, then set aside. Next, in a mixture of butter and olive oil, fry the minced beef with the paprika, allspice, chilli flakes, remaining garlic and some black pepper until the meat is well browned and cooked through. Season to taste with salt. Now add the chopped spinach to the meat – there is no need to add any liquid because spinach has a lot of water in it. Stir constantly until the spinach has wilted and is well mixed into the meat, then stir in the okra and spring onions. Tip the lot into a serving dish and eat with the yoghurt.

NOTE

If you want to make this dish more substantial you could, before frying the meat, fry a cupful of rice in olive oil until all the grains are well coated, then add the meat as above but this time, before you add the spinach, pour in a cup of water and cook the meat and rice together until the rice is done. Then continue by adding the spinach as above.

opposite page There is no such thing as a free cup of tea or Turkish coffee – you'll have to buy a carpet!

Lunch in the afternoon

Most mornings in summer I awake to a cacophonous dawn chorus created by the parrots that live in a huge aviary behind my bedroom. The sun rises late and I switch on the coffee machine, then Tess and I sit on the terrace sipping strong, aromatic *cafes solos*. Half a kilometre away lies the Mediterranean, like a cloth of black velvet in a jeweller's display case, scattered with handfuls of glinting diamonds. These are the lights of scores of small fishing boats heading back to the port of Estepona, with meagre catches of sardines, anchovies, squid, octopus, red mullet, dabs, shrimps, prawns and the occasional bass. Suddenly the sun is up, and across the date palms the Mediterranean turns from black to azure. The coffee machine hisses and splutters and I grind some more beans for another cup. As the sun climbs, you can see the Rift mountains of Morocco, and before the summer sea haze forms you can make out the Rock of Gibraltar. In our garden, with its luxuriant green foliage, huge bushes of red and white flowering oleanders surround the house. The figs are beginning to ripen, along with the apricots and peaches, although the oranges and lemons will not be ready until about Christmas. Chillies, peppers and coriander grow in tubs. We have bushes of rosemary and a bed of thyme.

below Puerto de la Duquesa.

My first job – aha, I do mean a job – before I grind the coffee beans is to switch on the sprinklers to water the garden. Once small rivulets of overflow trickle on to the terracotta-tiled terrace it is time to shower and dress and dream of the day to come…

… As we breakfast on a couple of eggs, cooked on the *plancha* with a drop of olive oil and seasoned with a dash of sherry vinegar, sea salt and ground black pepper, plus a slice of coarse country bread, the Spanish working man will be in a café breakfasting on country bread spread thick with paprika-flavoured pork dripping, possibly studded with tiny pieces of deep-fried caramelized garlic. He, too, will have a *cafe solo* but probably laced with rum or aniseed liqueur, or maybe just a straight glass of aniseed liqueur, before he heads off to the construction site or to the hills.

While Tess feeds the pets, I deadhead the geraniums. There is a screech from the kitchen garden, where we have a small pond. Tess has discovered a terrapin, about 8 inches in diameter, which has escaped from the pond and is attempting to attack the cat food in the kitchen. Pets fed, garden watered, terraces swept and truant terrapins returned to their rightful habitat, it is time to go to work. This involves poor Tess having to lift the laptop from the study on to the table in the covered terrace by the jacaranda trees. We spend two hours writing this or another book until about noon. If we top the morning with a *cafe solo* we tail it with a glass of iced fino sherry, a thin slice of manchego cheese, a couple of olives and a sliver of serrano ham before going down to the village – ostensibly to collect our post and the newspapers but in reality as an excuse to catch up on the gossip and have a few pre-lunch tapas at Bar Sebastian, the only truly authentic tapas bar between Gibraltar and the Cabo del Teresa. Inside, it is dark, cool and immaculately clean. In between preparing food, Maria, Sebastian's wife, embarks on the cleaning, immaculate in her smart dress and crisp white apron, rather like a gang of painters attacking the Forth Bridge.

After a couple of sherries, some octopus salad and some broad beans, we have to discuss with Fernando a supply of logs we require for the winter. We also have to arrange with Maria's elderly mother to make us some more chorizo and with Sebastian's uncle to bring us another large container of his cold-pressed olive oil. And then, of course, we have to plan lunch.

Tess wants to go to the Venta Coza on the road to Cassares, an imposing-looking conservatory perched on the side of the road where once, at the invitation of a passing farmer, she played with a young kid goat, which in brutal Spanish logic is a food source and not a pet. We sit down to eat at about 2.30pm. To start, we have a

crunchy salad of lettuce, sweet onions, green tomatoes, tuna fish, hard-boiled eggs and olive oil. Then I have fillets of salt cod cooked in a spicy tomato sauce and Tess has a grilled sole, studded with slivers of crisply fried garlic, with lemon juice and fresh wild asparagus mixed with scrambled eggs. After the fish course we have half a roast suckling pig served with just the roasting juices from the pan and a purée of carrots flavoured with saffron.

We finish lunch at about 5.15pm. It is still very hot, with a heavy haze hanging over the Mediterranean, and herds of bulls mooch disconsolately around the Cortigo (a farmhouse) looking in vain for shade. By the side of

the road, a shepherd sits in a cloak and wide-brimmed hat, keeping half an eye on his herd of goats. Two eagles soar high above the Andalusian campo as a Pegaso truck laden with massive blocks of Cassares stone grinds down the hill trailing a pall of white dust in the hot afternoon ...

I feel a gentle hand tap my face. It is my wife. 'Come on, get up,' she says. 'It's past eleven o'clock and that Spanish chapter has to be written today.' I stumble out of bed, take a couple of vitamin tablets, make a cup of Nescafe and write the introduction to this Spanish bit. Life's a bitch, isn't it!

The Greeks and the Turks have their mezze, the Spanish have tapas. *Tapa* means 'to cover' or 'a cover' and probably the first *tapa* ever served was a slice of country bread about the diameter of a wine glass, which, in the days before refrigeration and air conditioning, the thoughtful patron of a bar would give to thirsty workers to place over their glass of

wine or sherry to keep the flies out. Idly in conversation, they would nibble at the bread, and so a tradition unique to Spain was born.

Tapas can be anything: half a dozen olives, a slice of ham on a piece of bread, red peppers dry-roasted until the skin is black, then skinned and marinated in olive oil, chopped garlic and lemon juice. It could be half a dozen small clams, *almejas*, steamed open on the *plancha* under a small earthenware saucer. It could be a couple of meatballs in tomato sauce or a salad of cooked beans and potatoes, mixed with tuna fish, anchovies and hard-boiled eggs and lightly bound together with mayonnaise. It could be little *morcilla* – tiny black puddings – or cubes of fried potato spiced with paprika.

Little pieces of barbecued octopus with chopped raw onions, lemon juice and oil, or tiny shrimps or prawns cooked on a *plancha*, with crunchy, crystallized sea salt around them so you can eat the shells as well. Or a couple of spoonfuls of baby broad beans fried with a little diced serrano ham. Or a mini serving of chickpea and tripe soup flavoured with saffron. The list is absolutely endless. There is no room, sadly, in this book, to enlarge on this fascinating gastronomic phenomenon. Perhaps I will write a whole book on them one day.

Catalan broad bean salad

SERVES 4 - 6

1 kg/2¼lb	young broad beans (shelled weight)
1	hearty lettuce, such as Cos, finely shredded
2 tbsp	finely chopped fresh mint
about 200g/ 7oz	thinly sliced serrano or Parma ham, cut into very thin slivers

FOR THE DRESSING:

2	cloves of garlic, peeled
juice of 2	lemons
2 large tsp	sweetish mustard
1 tsp	sugar
	olive oil
	sea salt and black pepper

This and the two recipes that follow are typically Catalan, from the Barcelona region of Spain.

Blanch the broad beans in a large pan of boiling salted water for 2–3 minutes. Drain and leave to cool, then peel off the thin skin from each bean. Mix the beans with the lettuce, mint and ham and put into a salad bowl.

For the dressing, whack everything into a blender, gradually adding enough olive oil to give a fairly thick emulsion. Pour the dressing over the salad.

right The Holy Family Cathedral, Barcelona – unfinished masterpiece of architect Antonio Gaudí.

red peppers stuffed with salt cod purée

SERVES 6

6	small to medium red peppers
450g/1lb	fillet of salt cod, soaked in fresh water for at least 6 hours (buy a fillet that has neither bones nor skin, if possible)
6	cloves of garlic, peeled
600ml/1 pint	milk
	olive oil
1	small sachet of top-quality instant potato
	sea salt and black pepper

FOR THE SAUCE:

2	large red peppers
1	large clove of garlic, finely chopped
	olive oil
1 heaped tsp	paprika
1 cup	double cream

First place the red peppers, including the ones for the sauce, on a baking tray in a very hot oven – with no seasoning, no oil, no nothing, just the red peppers – and roast until the skins are black. Leave to cool, then pull off the stems, carefully remove the pith and pips inside and peel off the skin so that you have succulent little red pepper sacks. Coarsely chop the 2 large red peppers for the sauce and set aside.

Next cut the salt cod fillet into cubes, pop it into a saucepan with the garlic and milk, bring to the boil and simmer until the cod and garlic are tender. Strain the milk from the garlic and cod and put to one side. Now in a blender or food processor, purée the cod and garlic with a little of the milk to make a very stiff purée. With the blender going full blast, pour in a thin line of warm olive oil until you have a smooth, garlicky, oily purée. Taste and season if necessary. If the purée is too runny, which it can sometimes be, simply blend in a little of the instant potato.

Stuff the peppers with the fish purée, paint them lightly with olive oil and place in a medium-hot oven until they have warmed through.

For the sauce, fry the chopped garlic in a little olive oil, add the chopped red peppers and season with salt and pepper. Stir in the paprika and cook for 2–3 minutes. Stir in the cream and cook for another 2 minutes. Then whack the lot into the blender and purée it so that you have a spicy, peppery, cream sauce to go with your stuffed peppers.

partridges cooked in vinegar

SERVES 4

4	partridges
	olive oil
4	young carrots, scraped and cut in half lengthways
8	celery sticks, trimmed to the same size as the carrots
1	red and
1	white onion, finely sliced
1	large clove of garlic, finely chopped
2	bay leaves
1	sprig of fresh thyme
8	medium-hot chillies
1 litre/1¾ pints	white wine vinegar
8	crunchy spring onions, cut into batons the same length as the carrots
	sea salt and black pepper

Sauté the partridges in a little olive oil until they are brown on all sides. Remove from the pan and set to one side. Clean out the pan and, in a little olive oil, cook the carrots, celery, onions and garlic until they are very slightly browned. Now put the vegetables in a deep casserole, place the partridges on top, season with a little salt and pepper and add the bay leaves, thyme and chillies. Cover the partridges with the white wine vinegar, place in a hot oven and cook for 30–40 minutes. After about 30 minutes, check the partridges with a skewer to see if they are cooked; if they are, pop in the spring onions and leave them to cook for 5–6 minutes so they are still crunchy.

Because of the curious vinegar sauce the best way to eat this dish is after it has been left overnight in the refrigerator. The partridges benefit from the cold marinating and any fat will float to the surface and can be easily removed. Reheat gently to serve.

a Moorish Andalusian endive salad

The word Moorish is generally a clichéed term applied to a dish by someone who knows neither how to cook nor to eat, but this salad is Moorish because it uses spices like paprika, cumin and saffron, which the Arabs brought to Spain in the 9th century. You will have to play with the quantities to suit your own taste but the base of the sauce is tomato, olive oil and sherry vinegar. When it is finished it should look like tomato juice. So, let's experiment, and why not!

Take 4 skinned, deseeded and chopped tomatoes, half a tablespoon of paprika, half a tablespoon of ground cumin, a bloody great pinch of saffron and a good dash of olive oil and whizz it round in the blender. You have probably got a fairly thick goo, so now add a good dash of sherry vinegar and a bit more olive oil. Taste it, add some salt and pepper and see how you feel. Chill it before you use it and pour it over some crispy, crunchy endive leaves with a load of hard-boiled eggs cut in half.

PS: Once or twice a year, I dry some chillies, rosemary and thyme and stuff them into a litre bottle, which I then fill with best-quality virgin olive oil and leave for about 6 months. It is then ready to use for trickling over a pizza, sautéing prawns or whatever. I use it in this salad instead of plain olive oil.

black pudding **and sausages with almonds**

There are two divine sausages available where I live. One is a morcilla, which is a small black pudding often flavoured with onion, and the other is a chorizo, a spicy, pure pork sausage. This recipe is a perfect example of Hispano-Arab cuisine. It's a gutsy dish, makes you fart and is full of cholesterol – it's certainly one of my favourites!

The basics of the dish, per person, are one small black pudding, one small chorizo, one thin sliver of belly of pork and one boiled potato.

SERVES 4

4	potatoes
	olive oil
4	small black puddings, preferably morcilla
4	small chorizo
4	very thin slices of belly of pork (in Spain this is often salted and cured – it's even better if you can get that)
1	large onion
2	cloves garlic
50g/2oz	ground almonds
2 tbsp	chopped parsley
1	bay leaf
1	sprig of fresh thyme
	sea salt and black pepper

Boil the potatoes in their skins until they are almost cooked but still, as they say in foodie circles, *al dente*. Drain, return them to the hot saucepan, sprinkle with sea salt, then put the lid on and allow them to cool naturally. When they are cool, peel off the skins and put the potatoes to one side.

Put some olive oil in a large pan, prick the black puddings and chorizo and gently fry them in the oil. Once these have started cooking, add the belly of pork and cook on both sides until very slightly crisp. By this time the pan will contain a lot of red oil that has come out of the chorizo. Remove the sausages and pork from the pan and place in an ovenproof serving dish. Add the potatoes to the dish.

Now, in the oil left in the pan, fry the onions and garlic until they are completely cooked. Stir the ground almonds into the oil and cook for a few minutes. Now stir in about 150ml/¼ pint water, add the parsley, bay leaf and thyme, season with salt and pepper and cook until you have a smooth sauce. Add a little more water if necessary. Pour this over the sausages and potatoes, pop into a hot oven to reheat, then serve.

casserole of vegetables

The Spanish are not very good at cooking vegetables. All too often you get a horrible stir-fry of frozen mixed vegetables including Brussels sprouts, carrots, onions, swede and God knows what else – limp, flavourless, invariably cold and swimming in water. Curious because it doesn't half bugger up a perfectly cooked Dover sole! Spain does produce splendid vegetables but they are used to prepare dishes or soups, not as an adjunct to a piece of meat or a piece of fish, and are served as a meal in their own right. So, here's a good one. This will probably serve 4 to 6 people. I should point out that it is basically a dish of beans in tomato sauce with fresh vegetables added, so you could choose celery instead of artichoke hearts and spinach or chard instead of, or as well as, asparagus.

SERVES 4 - 6

500g/1lb 2oz	dried white beans, such as butterbeans or haricot beans
3	onions, coarsely chopped
½ cup	chopped fresh parsley, plus a few parsley sprigs
8	tomatoes, skinned, deseeded and finely chopped
	olive oil
2	cloves of garlic, finely chopped
1 heaped tbsp	ground cumin
2	bay leaves
1	bunch of asparagus
6	cooked or bottled artichoke hearts
	vegetable stock or water to cover
6	eggs
	sea salt and black pepper

Soak the white beans in cold water overnight, then drain and put in a pan with one of the chopped onions and the parsley sprigs. Cover with water, bring to the boil and cook until almost tender. Drain, remove the parsley sprigs and set the beans aside.

Fry the remaining onions and the tomatoes in olive oil, then add the garlic and season with salt and pepper. Stir in the ground cumin and cook for a couple of minutes until you have a bit of a paste. Now add the white beans, a bit more olive oil, the chopped parsley, bay leaves and the vegetables. Barely cover with vegetable stock or water – if you have cooked the artichokes yourself, use that liquid instead. Cook gently for about 15 minutes or so, until all the vegetables are tender, then carefully crack open the eggs and poach them in the vegetables.

lobster in chocolate sauce

SERVES 4

	olive oil
	butter
1	small onion, finely chopped
2	large cloves of garlic, finely chopped
2	large lobsters, cut in half while still alive – sorry but that's how it is, or you could substitute about 20–24 large raw peeled prawns
6	red chillies, finely chopped
5cm/2 inch	piece of root ginger, peeled and cut into very, very fine slivers
	dry sherry
1 cup	fresh orange juice
225g/8oz	bitter chocolate, grated into a powder on the fine holes of your cheese grater
	sea salt and black pepper

FOR THE SAFFRON RICE:

2 cups	rice
	olive oil
	a generous pinch of saffron
2 tbsp	toasted pine nuts (this is simply done by chucking them into a hot, dry frying pan and shaking them about until they are slightly golden)
2 tbsp	toasted split almonds
2 tbsp	toasted raisins

First cook the rice. Wash it in cold water, then rinse and drain well. Fry it for 2–3 minutes in some olive oil until each grain is well coated with oil. Add enough water to cover plus a little bit, then season with salt. Add the saffron, put a lid on the pan and cook for about 15 minutes or until the rice is tender. Stir in the toasted nuts and raisins.

For the lobster, heat a little olive oil and butter in a large frying pan and fry the chopped onion and garlic until soft. Place the lobsters in the pan, flesh-side down, and sauté until slightly golden, then turn them on to their shells and continue frying for 2 or 3 minutes, until the shells start to go pink. Season with salt and pepper, then add the chillies and ginger. Turn up the heat, add a dash of sherry and heat for a second or two, then flame it, standing well back. When the flames have died down, add a little more sherry and cook for another 5 minutes or so, until the lobster shells have become completely pink. Transfer the lobsters to a serving dish and keep warm. Still over a high heat, add the orange juice to the pan and let it bubble until it has reduced by at least a third. Then, over a low heat, whisk in the chocolate, followed by a knob of butter. Whisk until you have a smooth, spicy sauce which, curiously, does not taste of chocolate. Pour the sauce over the lobster and serve with the rice. To make the rice look smart, you could mould it into little domes, pyramids or whatever you like, with a coffee cup or timbale mould, then turn it out on to the serving plates.

grilled sardines

Even if you don't have access to a beach at the back of your garden or a small fire of vine roots, you can still replicate the authentic flavour of Andalusian-style sardines. All you have to do is this:

Put a good layer of coarse sea salt in a shallow tray. Cover the salt with sardines, then cover the sardines with more salt. Repeat until you have three layers of sardines. Leave in the fridge for 6 hours. When you come to grill the sardines, either on a barbecue or, as they do in Spain, on bamboo skewers pegged into the sand in front of the aforementioned vine root fire, simply ensure your barbecue, *plancha* or hot, dry frying pan is very hot. Take the sardines from the salt but don't brush off the excess. Grill the sardines for about 4 minutes a side and don't keep lifting them up to see if they're done because you will just break them and make them look messy. Have confidence and don't turn them over until you reckon they are a little bit burnt, a little bit golden, and the skin is studded with crystals of toasted salt. Then turn them over and cook the other side in the same way. Mediterranean people do not gut or fillet the sardines, by the way; they eat them whole.

tinto verano

The great southern Spanish drink, not to be confused with sangria, and not to be dismissed because it sounds common! If you want to enjoy your lunch on the beach under the Andalusian sun you don't want to mess about with expensive bottles of Rioja or high-alcohol cocktails like sangria.

Take a large tumbler, quarter fill it with ice, then squeeze in the juice of one lime, fill the glass to two-thirds with red wine and stir in some lemonade.

iced gazpacho

Gazpacho is basically a tomato soup. This liquid salad can be coarse and lumpy or puréed until smooth, then drunk from a glass like a Bloody Mary. I like both versions, but I'll give you my recipe for the chunky one. It's quite simple – if you want to drink it in a glass, just blend it further until you have a Bloody Mary consistency.

This amount will be enough for about 10–12 people; it keeps very well in the fridge.

SERVES 10-12

1 litre/1¾ pints	natural tomato sauce (the kind sold in those nice foil-lined boxes – check that it is pure, with no additives)
	ice cubes
	olive oil
	wine vinegar
2kg/4½lb	tomatoes, skinned, deseeded and finely chopped
1kg/2¼lb	total weight of finely chopped onions, peeled and deseeded cucumber, and chopped red peppers
5 or 6	cloves of garlic, peeled and chopped
	a handful of fresh tarragon leaves
2 tbsp	sugar
	sea salt and black pepper

Put the tomato sauce in a bowl and empty at least 2 trays of ice cubes into it. Into a large food processor or, better still, a large blender the size of a small outboard motor, put about half a cup of olive oil and half a cup of vinegar. Tip in the tomatoes, vegetables, garlic and tarragon and coarsely purée the lot. Now tip in the tomato sauce and ice cubes and continue whizzing until the ice has broken down and you have a lovely cold soup. At this stage, taste it to see if it needs a little more oil or vinegar. Add the sugar and plenty of salt and pepper and, if it's a bit too thick, blend in some more ice cubes. The ice cubes replace the water that you will find as an ingredient in many other recipes for this soup. Some people like to serve it with a little garnish of finely chopped raw peppers, onions, cucumber, fried croûtons, etc – that's up to you.

paella

No Spanish cook has the same recipe for paella as another. Paella is basically a rice dish, named after the large, round, shallow pan in which it is cooked. In inland Spain it is made with vegetables and rabbit or chicken. Along the coast it is more likely to be prepared with fish or shellfish, or a combination of both. It is truly a movable feast. Aficionados will tell you it must be cooked over a vine wood fire in the open air. This isn't strictly necessary but there are a couple of basic rules you must follow. The use of best-quality Spanish short grain rice is essential, as are first-quality olive oil and real saffron stamens. After that it's pretty much down to you what you put in it. There are some exquisite rice dishes simply cooked with squid ink and broad beans (this is not strictly a paella, although it is cooked in a paella, and is normally called *arroz con ...*, that is to say, rice with ...). Restaurants that offer *arroz* instead of paella tend to be quite serious and authentic because, it must be said, paella has become a bit of a catch-all dish – rather like the classic quiche Lorraine, which became bastardized by wine bars in the Seventies when it was thought that

anything cooked in a pastry case with cream was a quiche – not so!

I cook paella quite frequently in my garden, in a simple tin paella, 50cm/20 inches in diameter, over a huge portable gas ring. You can buy a tin like this from any hardware store in Spain for a couple of quid. The appropriately sized gas ring is also available for next to nothing and you can take it home with you after your next holiday!

A 50cm/20 inch paella dish will cook enough for about 10 people, and you will need the following ingredients:

right My outdoor kitchen

is a great place to cook.

SERVES 10

	olive oil
1	small chicken or rabbit, cut into bite-sized pieces, bones and all
5 or 6	cloves of garlic, finely chopped
2	large onions, finely chopped
1kg/2¼lb	Spanish short grain rice, washed, rinsed, drained and dried
6	large tomatoes, skinned, deseeded and chopped
2	red peppers, chopped
2	bay leaves
2	sprigs of fresh thyme
	a load of saffron
	fish stock, chicken stock or water to cover
1kg/2¼lb	mussels and/or clams, scrubbed
1kg/2¼lb	frozen petits pois
500g/1lb 2oz	fresh prawns in their shells
	sea salt and black pepper

First heat some olive oil in your pan and fry the chicken or rabbit until it is crisp on the outside. Then add the garlic and onions and stir around with the meat until they are soft. Then add the rice and stir it around until each grain is coated with oil. Season with salt and pepper. Next stir in the tomatoes and red peppers. Add the bay leaves, thyme and saffron and then pour in enough stock or water to cover the rice. Put some kind of makeshift lid on top – a sheet of aluminium or a clean dustbin lid will do – and cook gently until all the liquid has been absorbed. At this point the rice will not be quite cooked. Add the mussels and/or clams, the frozen peas and the prawns. Replace the lid. The natural juices from these ingredients will provide the extra liquid needed to finish cooking the rice. The dish is ready when the clams and mussels have opened. A well-cooked paella should have a crunchy crust on its bottom. The choice bits are the scrapings off the bottom of the pan.

fish baked in salt

This ubiquitous dish is one of the great ones of the Mediterranean, and of southern Spain in particular. But it is invariably totally ruined by being served with a spoonful of those soggy, nasty vegetables described on page 85 and possibly some hard-boiled or, worse still, tinned potatoes. Except in restaurants of the highest integrity, when ordering *Pescado a la Sal*, insist on having all the vegetables served separately, because the whole purpose of this method of cooking is to preserve the exquisite flavours of perfectly fresh fish. Other cultures have similar cooking methods – the Chinese use clay ovens, Romany gypsies cook hedgehogs in mud, and Polynesians wrap their food in leaves and bake it in the ground. I am sure those of you who remember the Robert Carrier cookery cards rushed out to buy a chicken brick in the late Sixties and early Seventies. The thing about this style of cooking is that the flavours are hermetically sealed inside and not diluted by poaching in water or evaporated in the oven.

It is important to have a good quantity of coarse rock salt and the fish must be brilliantly fresh. It must be whole, be it a bream or a bass, and it must weigh an absolute minimum of 900g/2lb. Gut the fish, then sprinkle a little salt inside with a sprig of parsley, a sprig of thyme and a couple of lemon wedges. Place the fish on a baking tray that has been covered with a layer of rock salt about 1cm/½ inch deep. Then completely cover the fish in a mound of salt and pat it down. Pop it into a very hot oven for about 25 minutes. The salt will form a hard crust, so to check whether the fish is done, plunge a skewer into the fish. Leave it for a moment or two then pull it out; if it is hot, the fish is cooked. Then begins the fun of chipping away the salt. Start around the edges of the fish and try and lift it off in one piece. Then, starting from the tail, try to peel off the skin in one piece. Carefully lift off the fillet, then lift out the backbone and remove the other fillet. Place on serving plates.

All you need now to enjoy this dish are some melted butter, a squeeze or two of fresh lemon juice and a little sprinkling of salt and pepper, because the salt that surrounded the fish during cooking will in no way have made it salty. A plate of Jersey new potatoes and a little crisp salad, followed by raspberries and clotted cream, a bottle of Meursault (bugger the *tinto verano!*) and you're in heaven.

far left One of scores of small fishing boats I watch each morning from my balcony – looks romantic, but catches are pitifully small.
left Fixing lines and nets in Estepona port.

93

left Jesus Gil, the flamboyant mayor of Marbella – dubbed as 'the last sultan?' by the Spanish press.

POSTCARD FROM SPAIN

Although closer to the Atlantic than the Mediterranean, Jerez is an essential part of Mediterranean culture. It is, of course, where the most exquisite of fine white wines, sherry, is produced. Sherry is not just about weddings and funerals, Dundee cake, and old ladies in hats, it is a fine, clear drink that prepares your palate for the fragrant, spicy food of this region.

There are several types of sherry, from extremely dry to very sweet. Here, in Andalusia, where I am lucky enough to live, fino is the preferred style. It is light, crisp and fresh, always served chilled, and goes well with anything. Then there is manzanilla, just a fraction sweeter than fino. Then you have the amontillado, which starts life as a fino but is aged in barrels until it develops an earthy taste. It is sometimes slightly sweet. On to the oloroso, which is rich and fruity and ruby in colour, then finally, of course, the famous cream sherry that we associate with weddings and funerals.

If you want a brilliant morning, ring up my chums at the Gonzales Byass *bodega* in Jerez and ask for a trip around the cellars. The complex is like a small village and has great historical and architectural interest. You will become

below My barrel in Gonzales Byass' hall of fame! (Slightly to the right of Mrs Thatcher, Ho! Ho!)

intoxicated by the aroma of sherry escaping through the huge oak barrels and experience a timeless artisanal tradition that is a million miles away from the lager louts of some of the less refined Mediterranean resorts. If they take you into what they call the hall of fame, you will see ancient barrels of sherry signed by opera singers, prime ministers, bull fighters, monarchs, presidents, princes, divas, racing drivers, soccer players and musicians. Look a little closer and you will find one barrel, slightly to the right of Margaret Thatcher, slightly to the left of the former president of Columbia and resting squarely on top of Winston

above Ronda bullring – heavy with atmosphere in the hot Spanish sun.

Churchill, with my signature! I am immensely proud that I was invited.

If you are still clearheaded after your trip around the *bodega*, take time to visit the Spanish School of Equitation, where the dancing horses perform, and enjoy the stirring display of passionate, macho horsemanship and the disciplined elegance of the magnificent Andalusian horses. The good thing is that when the show is over you still have time to leg it down the coast to Puerto de Santa Maria for lunch in one of the best restaurants in Spain, El Faro (the lighthouse). The chef and owner is called Fernando and, if the Michelin guide were not such a xenophobic publication and if it knew where Spain was, El Faro would certainly have two stars.

If you finish lunch at about 4.30pm, you might just get to Ronda in the late evening sun. To find the bullring, walk through the huge, arched door, more or less opposite Pedro Romero's restaurant, named after the famous bullfighter who was born

in 1755 and created the rules of classical bullfighting. He started fighting at eight years of age and died at 90, having killed 6,000 bulls. Whatever you think about the brutality of this classically Spanish theatre, just stand on the sand, gaze at the terraces and you will feel the whole of Spain engulf you like a Goya painting. And if the thought of *Death in the Afternoon* appals you, cross the street and have an iced fino in Pedro Romero's bar.

above I meet a young fan in the bullring.   **below** The Ronda landscape.

muscle beach mango delice

I was strolling along the beach in Estepona looking for a *chiringuito* for an early-evening aperitif, when I came across a beach bar called Muscle Beach, which to my horror specialized in fruit juices and health drinks (as well as, I must admit, some jolly tasty Italian food). But the idea of Muscle Beach, run by one Marco and his wife, Delice, is to provide fitness fanatics with an open-air gym, horror of horrors! After an abortive attempt at lifting one of the weights, I borrowed their bar for a few moments and made myself a fortifying cocktail, which I have dedicated to Delice.

For one person, take the chopped-up flesh of a large ripe mango, a couple of ice cubes, the juice of one fresh lime, a dash of coconut milk, a large dash of white rum and a dash of cane sugar syrup. Whack the lot into a blender. You can, of course, decorate it with exotic fruit if you want. After a couple of these you will see life, even on Muscle Beach, in a different way!

Of camels
and couscous

Morocco and Tunisia are the penultimate destinations in my journey around the Mediterranean. At times I have found myself confused, depressed and negative about the exotic locations that I am privileged to visit. So I would like to explain a few things.

After spending nearly eight months on the road, like a failed disciple to Damascus, I realize that I need some kind of culinary St Paul to convert me back to my original beliefs. Today I ate a sublimely moist leg of pork lacquered with golden, crispy crackling, with potatoes roasted in goose grease, Brussels sprouts, carrots, and gravy made from the vegetable cooking liquid and the pan juices from the pork. I thought, I must write a bit about Morocco and Tunisia, and I must talk about my journeys and the hotel lobbies in which I sit for hours.

I think it is time to go back some years. If there had not been Robert Carrier, Graham Kerr, Fanny Craddock and Philip Harben, people like me would not exist. Yet my enthusiasm for food was not inspired by these legendary people. It was inspired by my grandmother, who kept a pig, and by my Uncle Ken, who poached pheasants, snared rabbits and stole pigs. It was bred from chilly mornings, purple fingered, picking purple sprouting broccoli in the frost of a January Somerset garden. My interest in food stemmed from a simple bamboo fishing rod my father made using waxed twine from my grandfather's boot shop. And when, one day, I returned with a basket full of trout, caught on red worms that lived in the compost heap of my grandparents' garden, we had to look in the *Observer*'s book of fish to work out what they were. I cleaned and gutted them, asked my mother to make batter, then deep-fried them. I was 13 years old.

Fired with enthusiasm for cooking, my sister and I would pinch tomatoes from the garden, late at night after our parents had gone to bed, stuff them with parsley, breadcrumbs and cheese and roast them for a midnight feast. We had recently progressed from liquid Camp coffee in a bottle to instant coffee. With an inkling of an idea that there was something called espresso coffee, I discovered a method of making it: put a teaspoonful of Nescafé, a teaspoonful of sugar and a dash of cold water in a cup, spend 15 minutes grinding them to a paste with the back of a teaspoon, then pour on boiling water and, by some bizarre chemical process, a thick cream would appear on top of strong black coffee.

below A little night
shopping in the el-Fna
market, Place de Djemaa,
Marrakech.

above Amazing dates.

Right now I am sitting in an airport lounge with an armed guard at my side and a gofer to take care of my suitcases. Soon I will be sitting in a hotel lobby – maybe the Sheraton in Marrakech, maybe the Hilton or the Intercontinental in Tunis. Colourful destinations, exotic food, mysterious souks, and big signs on the long, straight boulevard outside my hotel, where camels graze or sit, bored, lifeless, on the desert strip beneath the sign that says 'Pizza Hut, 300 metres'. Because I live in Spain, some days I climb on to a boat and go to Morocco for lunch. Maybe to Ceuta, or Tétouan. And in Tétouan, in the old Medina (purists would not put old in front of Medina), I might walk through the narrow, arcaded passages, buy a hand-woven

silk carpet and eat a brochette of merguez (a spicy beef sausage, common throughout North Africa). I might drink a slightly dirty glass of pungent, fragrant, refreshing mint tea, or have a bowl of couscous, although, sadly, I would probably find a better one in Aix-en-Provence, or Sète, or any part of the French Mediterranean coast where the *pieds-noirs* installed themselves to cook North African food after the decolonization of Tunisia and Morocco.

Morocco and Tunisia are littered with relics of empire. Decrepit grand hotels, where Churchill or de Gaulle once stayed. Street names may be written in Arabic now but they still use the blue enamelled French plaques. You will still find the *place des putain*s, the *place de Gaulle* and the *rue d'épices*. You will, of course, discover agreeable people living in disturbing squalor.

Today, after my roast pork, I flipped through the travel pages of the *Mirror*, the *Mail*, the *Express*, the *Observer* and *The Times* and read at least twice that all villages and towns in Morocco and Tunisia are painted white. In fact the sprawling, crumbling city of Marrakech is a dirty oxblood colour which the tourist board calls pink. The other cities, towns and villages are made of cement or grey dung.

As something of an old fart, who in the late Sixties and early Seventies was too busy trying to cook the correct *boeuf à la bourguignonne*, or beat out chicken

below Marrakech.

above Street food at el-Fna market, Marrakech.

breasts without damaging them so the garlic butter would not escape when I sautéed my chicken Kiev, I never had the time or money to follow my friends of independent means when they took the Marrakech express. In the huge city centre they smoked dope, wore 'ban' banners and ate interesting food – deep-fried aubergines, merguez, kebabs, couscous – in the square that throbs in the middle of the Moroccan night, where snake charmers, contortionists, beggars and whores glide.

When I eventually went there I was a little disappointed, but just behind the mosque, the one with the huge minaret, next to the AT&T office, quite close to a shabby American Express bureau and a flyblown window full of pumps, starter motors

and assorted mechanical bric-a-brac, there is an extraordinary restaurant called La Fesse au Safran. You have to be courageous to pass the tea shops and coffee shops and run through the mayhem traffic but, once inside, you step into 1933. There is a cool, tiled, Arab Art Deco lobby. A man in a bottle-green dinner jacket greets you. He is, unbelievably, called Henri Balthazar. He walks with a limp and a slightly hunched shoulder and takes you to a table covered with a crisp damask cloth. Unfortunately, I am recognized by a Dutch couple sitting at the adjacent table, who happen to be residents of Marrakech and regular customers of the restaurant. After much chatter and almost cringe-making explanations, I am invited into the kitchen, where a serene lady called Carmel, sporting incongruous purple nail varnish, is stuffing pigeon breasts, almonds, fruit and

above left and *below*

Moroccan tagines.

nuts between handwoven layers of filo pastry. This is an elaborate, typically Moroccan speciality called *bisteeya* – a layered pie, partly savoury and partly sweet, usually finished off with a coating of sugar and cinnamon and baked until crisp. Exotic and exquisite. A man in dirty chef's whites is cursing the boys who scurry through the kitchen with steaming decorated earthenware tagines. In Morocco a tagine is a slowly simmered stew flavoured with preserved lemons, saffron, cumin, ginger and paprika. It takes its name from the pointed earthenware pot in which it is cooked and, confusingly, is quite different from the Tunisian tagine, which is a baked egg dish with vegetables or meat in it, like a solid soufflé or a fat omelette.

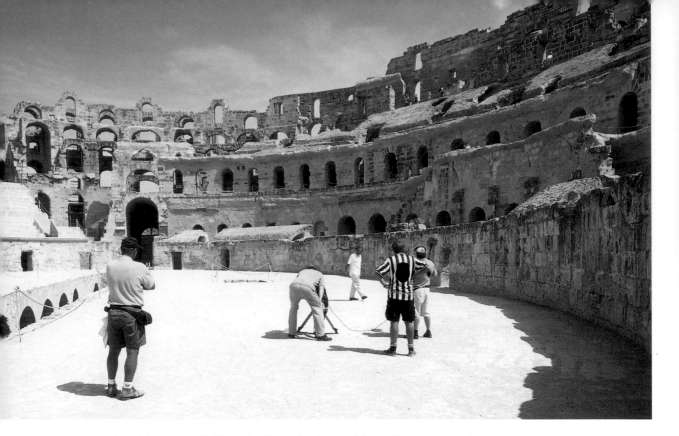

An old man, probably only 40 but he looks old, is piling couscous into ornate dishes. Couscous is the national dish of Morocco and revered as one of the great dishes of the world, along with the French bouillabaisse and coq au vin, the light and fluffy Yorkshire pudding, the Japanese sukiyaki and the Spanish paella, to mention but a few. The classic way to cook this dish is in a couscousière, a two-tiered affair where the couscous cooks in the flavoured steam of the stew below for a couple of hours. However, the availability of instant couscous makes it much easier to prepare (see recipe opposite).

above The coliseum in El Jem, Tunisia.

below I'm spoilt for choice in this wonderful Sousse market.

The next day, I am standing in the coliseum in El Jem in Tunisia. In this extraordinary amphitheatre, smaller but more complete than the one in Rome, I walk around the lion cages, through the tunnels where the Christians and slaves were caged before their inevitable, brutal death. Underneath a cloudless sky, in one of the world's greatest historical monuments, I fry a brik on my cranky old gas ring – a sliver of semolina flour pastry stuffed with an egg. I feel like writing a sweeping novel called *Lunch in the Afternoon*, in my view a great title for a book.

lamb couscous
with vegetables

SERVES 10

250g/9oz	chickpeas, soaked in water for 8 hours
1.5–2kg/3¼–4½lb	couscous
1kg/2¼lb	young carrots
1kg/2¼lb	young turnips
1kg/2¼lb	young courgettes
1kg/2¼lb	stewing lamb or mutton, cut into cubes
4	large onions, coarsely chopped
6	tomatoes, coarsely chopped
3–4	chillies, chopped, or
1 heaped tsp	chilli paste
1 tbsp	ground coriander
	a large knob of butter
	a big pinch of saffron
300g/11oz	raisins
	sea salt and black pepper

When cooking stews from North African countries, if the recipe says to add water, you could make it much richer and more luscious by using a combination of milk and water.

Drain the chickpeas, then put them in a pan, cover with fresh water and simmer until almost tender. Prepare the couscous according to the instructions on the packet. Scrape or peel the carrots and turnips and cut to the size of the courgettes.

Put the meat into a large saucepan with the chickpeas and all the other ingredients except the carrots, turnips, courgettes, couscous and raisins. Barely cover with water, bring to the boil and simmer for about 1 hour. Half way through this time add the carrots; 10 minutes later add the turnips, and then a few minutes later the courgettes. Season with salt and pepper.

Make a mound of the couscous in a warm serving dish and cover with the vegetables and meat, a little of the cooking liquid and the raisins. Serve the rest of the cooking liquid, or bouillon as it should be called, separately.

above and ***left*** The colourful tile work of what was once a mosque, in the old town of Marrakech.

right Natural good humour from fishermen resigned to the disappointment of small catches after long hours at sea.

Brik

Brik is a crisp, deep-fried pancake that is extremely popular in Tunisia as an
hors d'oeuvre or snack. It is a relative of the Chinese spring roll and won
ton. In its simplest form, you lay out a disc of pastry, break an egg into the
centre, smear some of the egg white around the edges, then fold it in half,
squeeze the edges together for a half-moon shape and drop it into deep hot
oil for a few seconds. You munch through this deliciously light pancake to a
soft egg inside. You can, of course, use other fillings. A particular favourite
is a mixture of flaked tinned tuna fish, a few chopped capers, spring onions
and parsley, as well as the egg. Or you could use an egg, some grated
cheese and chopped ham, or egg, cream cheese and chives. Brik is usually
served with a little shredded crisp lettuce and a wedge of lemon.

You may be able to find the pastry, a very thin semolina flour dough, in
some specialist delicatessens, sold in packets of 10 or 12 discs, about
20cm/8 inches in diameter. If not, filo can be substituted.

Later that night, we find ourselves in a hand-painted, pale-blue 1953 Buick rolling up the desert road to a small village called El Ttit. Our driver and guide takes us to what can only be described as an oasis of culinary civilization – an elegant, single-storied restaurant called Le Nichon d'Orée, run by a massive, shaven-headed bull of a man called Leon and his Tunisian wife. Leon must be something left over from the French foreign legion, who has gone native (no disrespect intended but he is a Beau Geste sort of man). They serve me meat in a rich gravy. It is very good and when, much later, we talk he explains that it is flavoured with coffee (see recipe on page 113).

sauté of beef, Leon's way

This is very similar to a Moroccan tagine but, and I don't wish to confuse you, dear reader, a Tunisian tagine is a baked egg dish which can resemble a Spanish omelette or a soufflé filled with vegetables or meat.

1kg/2¼lb	flank or shin of beef, cut into cubes
	a knob of butter
1	clove of garlic, finely chopped
3 coffeespoons	ground caraway seeds
3 coffeespoons	ground cumin
2–3 tbsp	tomato purée
1	cinnamon stick
2–3 tbsp	very finely ground espresso coffee
	sea salt and black pepper
TO GARNISH:	chopped spring onions or finely sliced red onion
	chopped fresh parsley or coriander

Fry the meat in the butter until well seared on all sides. Reduce the heat and add the garlic, caraway and cumin. Stir well so that the meat is covered with the spices, then season with salt and black pepper. Next stir in the tomato purée, add the cinnamon stick and enough water just to cover the meat. Stir thoroughly for a moment or two until the sauce begins to boil, then reduce the heat and add the coffee. Simmer gently for at least 1 hour or until the meat is very tender and the sauce has reduced to a thickish consistency.

Garnish with chopped raw spring onions or very thin slices of red onion and parsley or coriander.

mechouia

This Tunisian dish is basically a salad of peppers, tomatoes and onions that have been roasted or grilled, then chopped up and mixed with lemon juice and olive oil. There are many variations and it can manifest itself as a rather sour, grey purée or an elegantly prepared plate of stunningly contrasting flavours. This is my way. It is a cross between a salad niçoise and a ratatouille.

6	red and green peppers
4	large tomatoes
2	sweet onions
2–3	chillies, deseeded and finely chopped
1	whole pickled lemon rind, finely diced (see opposite)
2	celery sticks, cut into 2.5cm/1 inch batons
	a handful of chopped fresh parsley
1 tbsp	chopped capers
1 tsp	ground coriander
	olive oil
	lemon juice
1	small tin of anchovy fillets in olive oil, drained
1	small tin of tuna in olive oil, drained
6	eggs, hard-boiled and cut into quarters

Roast the peppers, tomates and onions in a hot oven until blackened and tender (note that the onions will take longer than the tomatoes and peppers). Leave to cool, then remove the skin and, in the case of the peppers and tomatoes, the pith and seeds. Chop into pieces about 2.5cm/1 inch square.

Carefully mix the onions, tomatoes and peppers together, then add the chillies, pickled lemon rind, celery, parsley, capers and ground coriander. Season to taste with olive oil and lemon juice. Tip on to a serving plate or dish and arrange the anchovy fillets, flaked tuna and hard-boiled eggs on top.

preserved lemons

Lemons preserved in salt are an indispensable part of North African cuisine. They are used in kebabs, chicken stews, lamb tagines and salads. You can buy them in specialist shops but they are easy to prepare at home.

Wash and dry the lemons and cut a couple of deep incisions in each one. Press sea salt into the incisions and around the lemons (as a guide, you will need about 100g/4oz sea salt to 1kg/2¼lb lemons). Put them into a wide-necked earthenware or Kilner-type jar, packing them in very tightly, and if possible put a weight on top of the lemons. Seal the jar and keep in a cool place for about a month before use. When you add the lemons to a dish, cut off and discard the pulp, using only the rind.

above Assembling the mechouia in the splendid coliseum at El Jem, Tunisia.

lamb tagine with prunes

SERVES 6 – 8

500g/1lb 2oz	stoned prunes
	honey
	butter
1	shoulder of lamb, boned and cut into bite-sized pieces
2	onions, finely diced
2–4	cloves of garlic, finely chopped
1½	teaspoons ground ginger
1½	teaspoons ground coriander
	a big pinch of saffron strands
1 tbsp	tomato purée
1	cinnamon stick
4	tomatoes, finely chopped
20	small shallots or silver-skinned onions, peeled
½ cup	sliced almonds, toasted
	sea salt and black pepper

Soak the prunes in water for 1 hour and then cook gently in the soaking water with a little honey until tender.

Heat some butter in a large pan, add the meat and fry until sealed on all sides. Add the onions and garlic and cook until golden. Next, stir in the ginger, coriander, saffron, tomato purée and cinnamon stick. Season with salt and pepper and add the chopped tomatoes. Cook over a low heat for 5–10 minutes and then pour in enough water to cover. Add the bone from the shoulder of lamb and simmer gently for 30 minutes.

In another pan, fry the shallots in butter until golden. Add them to the main dish and continue cooking until the lamb is tender. It should be a thick, rich, spicy stew. If there is too much liquid, boil until reduced. Stir in the prunes and honey, transfer to a serving dish and sprinkle over the toasted almonds.

Mummies, molokhia
& monuments

In my mind's eye, Cairo is one of those legendary cities – ancient, exotic, intriguing, romantic, glamorous and squalid. Like, say, Istanbul, it occupies a significant position between East and West and, indeed, North and South. A colossus of a city, spawned by the waters of the River Nile and honed and shaped by 7,000 years of civilization. I picture grand boulevards and fine colonial buildings, legacies of the French and British. There will be grand but faded hotels, originally built for the Grand Tour and the dilettante aristocratic Egyptologists (and Americans too, of course, who plundered the country in the name of art). There will be mysterious souks and markets redolent of cinnamon, cumin, coriander, saffron, pepper and all manner of spices. There will be stalls of exotic fruit and vegetables, there will be mountains of dates and pomegranates, there will be dark cafés, with Art Deco metal tables and chairs glinting beneath a slowly rotating ceiling fan, where you sip sweet, strong Turkish coffee, maybe smoke a water pipe or nibble on an exotic, honey-sweet pastry of cashew nuts and dried fruit. And, of course, there will be fine, faded and probably shambolic old restaurants, where colonial France melts, gastronomically speaking, into the Orient.

There will be old-fashioned department stores where purchases of cotton shirts are packed in tissue in sombre cardboard boxes, where change for a proffered note returns via a hissing and puffing tube linked to a plate-glass cash office somewhere in the bowels of the building. At night, a huge desert moon will glint on the Nile and occasionally freeze the lantine sail of a dhow gliding inexorably through the shimmering waters of Africa's greatest river. And if, as some say, the Mediterranean was the cradle of civilization, then surely the Nile must have been the hand that rocked it. The Nile, where the ancient Egyptians grew the first wheat, made the first beer and constructed cities and monuments and a civilization of agriculture, mathematics and science

unparalleled in the history of mankind.

In reality, though, modern Cairo is a dump. It is a squalid, festering mountain of derelict, half-completed mud-brick tenements. The Nile looks like some aborted canalization you might find in the Ukraine. My shiny, beaten-up Peugeot taxi is trapped in a fishnet of traffic jams, where the badly driven taxis lie like a shoal of sharks, waiting for the only exit in the congested street. At the junction to my left there is a battered, blue, four-wheel-drive truck crammed with black-uniformed, machine-gun-toting soldiers. A forlorn, fat, white-uniformed policeman stands helplessly under a sunshade blowing a whistle. On the grubby pavement that runs alongside the Nile, a man, watched by half a dozen passers-by, is kicking a woman, who is lying cradling her head in her arms. The traffic moves again to a symphony of horn blowers. It is early dusk. My throat burns from the acrid hot air that wafts over me through the unclosable window of the car. There is a putrid stench of urine and rotting vegetables.

My driver, Mohammed (who, I was later to find out, as he was with me for days, was the best driver in Cairo), saw a gap in the traffic, accelerated past a dead horse and swung into the immaculate drive of the Conrad Hilton, where a smiling, rotund gentleman in a fez opened the door and ushered us into the serene cool of the marble-floored atrium. We were courteously checked for guns and knives, although they took no notice of the pings that erupted from the machine as we walked through the metal detector and up the grand circular staircase to the dimly lit bar, where a thimbleful of Scotch cost a modest ten English pounds.

above Professor or/and
Dr Zahi Hawass,
Egyptologist extraordinaire!

POSTCARD FROM CAIRO

Monday

Hosted by the Egyptian Tourist Board, accompanied by plain-clothed armed police and escorted by soldiers, our motley caravan of five vehicles, carrying crew, directors, producers *et al*, ground its way through the outer slums of Cairo to the Pyramids and a meeting with an illustrious professor, who clicked into his well-oiled, highly polished discourse on the Pyramids. Apparently the builders were not slaves. They had a robust diet of many different kinds of bread, grilled salted fish, beer and the occasional pig. The Pharaohs ate soft fruit, vegetables, fish and cattle, but not pork because it was for the poor. The professor took us to a block, once again only half constructed and certainly very dilapidated, and led us into a storeroom littered with broken typewriters, bits of foam mattress, broken office furniture, a battered filing cabinet and a few cartons of bric-a-brac. A low-watt bulb hung by an ancient flex from the peeling ceiling. Two or three mummies were propped around the room, and in a large wooden crate was the perfect mummy of an Egyptian architect, who had died of natural causes at the age of 35, 3,000 years ago. 'We call him Mr and Mrs X,' said the learned doctor. 'I like him because he looks like the mummy from the film of the same name.'

'What will you do with him now?' I asked.

'Oh, I don't know,' he said. 'Maybe I'll take him back to his tomb. He's probably missing it by now.' Looking at his watch, he declared he had run out of time. There was another film crew outside in the corridor, awaiting his exclusive interview. Mike Connor, our director, kindly allowed them to use our film lights since they had none of their own. I wandered off and gazed, underawed, at the Pyramids in their shabby, scruffy, hot, dusty setting, then went in search of a coffee or a drink of some

above I'd rather a Silk Cut

any day!

kind. Nothing was available. While we rounded up the cars we watched a couple of camel drivers having a fight, admired the magnificent temporary theatre being built to stage Verdi's opera, *Aïda*, at the cost of millions and made a mental note never to believe those magnificent photographs in travel books and advertisements ever again.

right Sadly, the horses are

not always as well cared for

as the carts.

POSTCARD FROM
ALEXANDRIA

Wednesday

Travelled from Cairo to Alexandria by train, which dragged itself punctually through a squalid landscape featuring occasional vignettes of neat cornfields, weeping willows, buffalo and children swimming in the filthy river. At Alexandria Station, a decrepit but magnificent Moorish Art Deco edifice built in 1925, we were greeted like royalty by the ever-courteous Egyptians. More armed guards, more charming men and women from the Egyptian Tourist Board. We swept along the magnificent corniche, with its high Italianate buildings to the left, the azure-blue Mediterranean to the right. Past the hotels where Rommel and Churchill stayed, past a magnificent tomb to the unknown warrior, brilliantly misconstrued by my research team as a monument to the German and British soldiers of the battle of El Alamein, which was in fact some 70 kilometres further on. I casually mentioned that it seemed odd for a monument to a European battle to have Arabic inscriptions and be guarded by Egyptian soldiers. Whoops! That's television for you.

below Proof of illegal turtle trafficking – so vehemently denied!

We checked into a miserable hotel and set off for the market with the intention of buying turtles, which are sold illegally, against the Egyptian conservation constitution, so that we could release them back into the sea. Our ever-smiling, genuinely friendly guides explained that since it was illegal to sell turtles for food there could not be any in the market, and therefore we could not film something that did not exist. Catch 22.

Of the many famous sons and daughters of Alexandria, probably the most famous is the actor, bridge and backgammon player, Omar Sharif, but I would be surprised if even he wanted to return to the once-spectacular city of Alexandria. I, for one, never will.

above Life on the banks of the Nile can be fun for kids ...

POSTCARD FROM LUXOR

Friday

We are really looking forward to heading south and down the Nile. We drive in air-conditioned cars through impeccable countryside, with neat strips of cotton, maize, wheat, peppers, tomatoes and sesame seeds, past the Nile which, in a bizarre way, looks not unlike the Thames in Sonning. We overtake trotting, well-fed donkeys pulling laden carts with tyred wheels, and gleaming horses pulling highly polished carriages. There are no mountains of garbage, muck and polystyrene cans, and although it is very hot the air smells sweet and the belly of the mother Nile is pregnant with ripe fertility. We check into the Winter Garden Hotel, which in fact is two hotels the old colonial building, slavishly maintained to the standards of yesteryear, and the new Winter Garden, a cheerful,

above ... with dreams,

right ... but life gets a lot harder later.

bubbling, efficient, all-purpose hotel, with friendly staff, a bartender who does not use a measure and a coffee shop that serves middle-of-the-road local and international food 24 hours through 24 happy hours a day.

The temple at Luxor is simply outstanding, but don't visit after ten in the morning or you will fry in the reflected heat. No one can tell you how it was built, and in fact you don't need to know. It is just there and it is just remarkable.

right The magnificent temple at Luxor.

Sunday

We motor past the factories of Alabaster and the mud-brick villages that blend into the arid brown, or occasionally ochre, sand hills to the temple of Queen Hatshepsut, known to us hoi polloi as Queen Tomato Ketchup. The Egyptians are intensely proud of the magnificent restoration of this extraordinary temple. However, approached from a distance, it looks to me like the council offices of Stroud, carefully built in Bath stone.

It was here in 1997 that gunmen ran down the gullies in the surrounding hills and opened fire. It is a savage, sad and magnificent arena which, despite my cynical observations, you should take time out to visit and consider what humane and philosophical qualities the Egyptians must have to cope with their heritage and survive so magnanimously and kindly in the brutal and deprived world in which they now find themselves.

above The Egyptians are a friendly lot; in the background is Queen Hatshepsut's Temple.

left Q. "... and why is your wife walking behind?"
A. "She hasn't got a donkey."

127

egyptian fish tagine

900g/2lb	firm white fish fillets (bass for preference), skinned and cut into 4cm/1½ inch squares
	olive oil
	lemon juice
	saffron strands
2	green peppers, coarsely chopped (smaller than the fish pieces)
2	onions, coarsely chopped
3–4	cloves of garlic, crushed
	groundnut oil
450ml/15fl oz	tomato passata
1 tsp	dried chilli flakes
1 tsp	ground cumin
	flour
	sea salt and black pepper

Put the fish in a shallow dish and marinate in olive oil and lemon juice with a pinch of saffron for 30 minutes–1 hour.

Fry the peppers, onions and garlic in groundnut oil until they are almost cooked but still a little crunchy. Now add the tomato passata, stir in the chilli flakes, cumin and a large pinch of saffron and season with salt and pepper. Cook until the sauce has reduced by about a fifth and is rich and spicy. Put to one side, or even prepare ahead and leave in the fridge until you wish to use it.

Dry the fish pieces and dredge them in flour seasoned with salt and pepper (if you can, put some more saffron in the flour, too). Quickly fry the fish pieces in hot oil until they are slightly crisp and golden on the outside but still raw inside. Put half the tomato and pepper sauce into a shallow ovenproof dish, arrange the fish pieces on top, cover with the remaining sauce and bake for about 15 minutes in an oven preheated to 200°C/400°F/Gas Mark 6.

braised okra

1	large onion, finely chopped
2	cloves of garlic, finely chopped
	butter
1½ tsp	ground cardamom
1 tsp	grated nutmeg
1kg/2¼lb	okra, stems removed
350ml/12fl oz	tomato passata
2	bay leaves
4	tomatoes, skinned, deseeded and diced
	a handful of chopped fresh coriander
	sea salt and black pepper

Fry the onion and garlic in butter until golden, then stir in the cardamom and nutmeg. Add the okra, tomato sauce and bay leaves, season with salt and pepper and then simmer for about 15 minutes or until the okra is cooked (the sauce will be quite glutinous because of the okra). Just before serving, stir in the chopped tomatoes and coriander.

rice with prawns **and chickpeas**

at least 20	large raw prawns, shell on
	groundnut oil
1	onion, finely chopped
4	cloves of garlic, crushed
1 tsp	ground cumin
1½ tsp	ground cardamom
6	small red chillies, deseeded and finely chopped
2–3 cups	short grain rice such as Arborio, rinsed and drained
4	tomatoes, skinned, deseeded and chopped
about 1 litre/ 1¾ pints	chicken stock
300g/11oz	cooked chickpeas
	juice of 2 lemons
1	bunch of fresh dill or coriander, coarsely chopped
	sea salt and black pepper

Remove the head and shell from each prawn and cut down the back so that they will open up like butterflies when cooked. With the point of the knife, remove the thin black intestinal vein that runs down the back of the prawns. Set the prawns aside.

Heat some groundnut oil in a large shallow pan – a paella pan would be ideal – and fry the onion and garlic until golden. Add the cumin, cardamom and chillies. Next stir in the rice until it is well mixed with the onion, oil, garlic and spices. Then stir in the chopped tomatoes and add enough chicken stock to cover. Give all the ingredients a final stir and season with salt and pepper to taste. Cover and cook over a low heat for about 20 minutes or until all the liquid has been absorbed and the rice is cooked. Stir in the chickpeas and keep warm.

Heat some more groundnut oil in a frying pan over a high heat. Stir-fry the prawns just for a minute or two, until they turn pink and open out. Season with salt, pepper and the lemon juice, then toss on to the rice. Sprinkle with the chopped dill or coriander and serve.

Egyptian green soup

The essential ingredient for this refreshing soup is a large quantity of finely chopped molokhia leaves. These are, of course, easily available in Egypt but you will probably have to make do with dried ones from a Middle Eastern food shop. The leaves have glutinous properties (so you could use finely chopped okra as an alternative), giving the soup a pleasing texture that is not dissimilar to Chinese shark's fin soup.

below One wing of Queen Hatshepsut's temple. From a distance it looks more like council offices in Stroud but, although over-restored, it's well worth a (quick) visit.

4	cloves of garlic, finely chopped
4	red chillies, deseeded and finely chopped
	butter
1 tsp	cayenne pepper
1 tbsp	ground coriander
at least 450g/1lb	fresh molokhia leaves, finely chopped
1 cup	finely chopped fresh parsley
1 cup	finely chopped fresh coriander
1 litre/1¾ pints	chicken stock or water
	sea salt and black pepper

In a large saucepan, fry the garlic and chillies in butter and then stir in the cayenne pepper and ground coriander. Next add the molokhia leaves, parsley and fresh coriander. Stir in the stock or water, bring to the boil and simmer for about 15 minutes. Season to taste with salt and pepper, then serve.

If you can only get dried molokhia, use 50g/2oz, crush the leaves with your hands, then soak them in a little hot water until doubled in size.

tahini sauce

This makes a delicious accompaniment to kebabs or grilled fish or meat.

juice of 2–3	lemons
	a dash of white wine vinegar
1½ tsp	finely crushed caraway seeds
2	cloves of garlic, very finely chopped
225g/8oz	tahini (sesame seed paste)
	sea salt

Pour a cup of water into a saucepan, add the lemon juice, vinegar, caraway seeds and garlic and heat gently. Over a low heat, whisk in the tahini until you have a smooth, creamy sauce. Season to taste with salt and serve tepid over sizzling kebabs.

baked fish
stuffed with rice and dates

When ordering your fish, ask the fishmonger to remove the backbone from the inside, leave the head and tail on but remove all other fins and descale if necessary.

1	whole fish, such as salmon or bass, weighing at least 1.25kg/2½lb after gutting
juice of 2	lemons
1½ cups	chopped dates
4	pieces of crystallized ginger, finely chopped
½ cup	ground almonds
2–3 cups	cooked rice (the exact quantity will depend on the size of your fish)
1 heaped tsp	ground cinnamon
	butter
2	lemons or **4** limes, cut into wedges
	sea salt and black pepper

Rub the cavity of the fish well with the lemon juice and some salt and pepper. To make the stuffing, mix together the dates, ginger, ground almonds, rice and cinnamon. Push 6–8 hazelnut-sized knobs of butter into the mixture and stuff the fish with it.

Butter a large piece of aluminium foil, smother the fish itself in butter and season with salt and pepper. Wrap tightly in the foil, place on a baking tray and bake for 30–40 minutes in an oven preheated to 200°C/400°F/Gas Mark 6. To check if the fish is cooked, push a skewer into it and leave it there for a moment or two; if the skewer is warm or hot when you withdraw it, the fish is done. Serve the fish with warm melted butter and wedges of lemon or lime.

tabbouleh

One of the most refreshing, mouth-tingling salads to come out of North Africa. It is amazingly simple, and you can adjust the quantities to suit your own taste if necessary.

4 cups	bulgar wheat
1 cup	skinned, deseeded and finely chopped tomatoes
1 cup	mixed finely chopped spring onions and red onion
1 cup	chopped fresh coriander
1 cup	chopped fresh parsley
½ cup	finely chopped fresh mint
2–3	cloves of garlic, very finely crushed
at least 1 cup	lemon juice
at least ½ cup	good olive oil
	sea salt and black pepper

Prepare the bulgar wheat according to the instructions on the packet. Combine all the ingredients in a salad bowl and serve chilled.

sauté of chicken
with lemon and turmeric sauce

1	corn-fed chicken, jointed into 4 portions
	groundnut oil
2	onions, finely diced
4	cloves of garlic, crushed
4 heaped tbsp	ground turmeric
1½ tsp	ground cumin
1½ tsp	ground coriander
600ml/1 pint	fresh lemon juice
6	tomatoes, finely chopped
2	cups cooked chickpeas
	a handful of finely chopped fresh coriander
	sea salt and black pepper
	yoghurt mixed with chopped fresh mint, to serve

Fry the chicken pieces in groundnut oil until they are crisp and golden, then stir in the onions and garlic and continue cooking until they begin to colour. Season with salt and pepper. Now stir in the turmeric, cumin and coriander and make sure the chicken pieces are well coated with the spices. If this concoction is very dry, add a little more oil, as you must gently cook the spices for another 5 minutes, stirring all the time, without burning. Now add the lemon juice and stir it in well. It should just cover the chicken; if it doesn't, add a little water to compensate. Stir in the chopped tomatoes and simmer gently for about an hour, until you have a smooth sauce coating the chicken pieces. Add the cooked chickpeas and chopped coriander and warm through. The flavours of the lemon and turmeric will be softened delightfully by the addition of a dollop of mint-flavoured yoghurt just before serving.

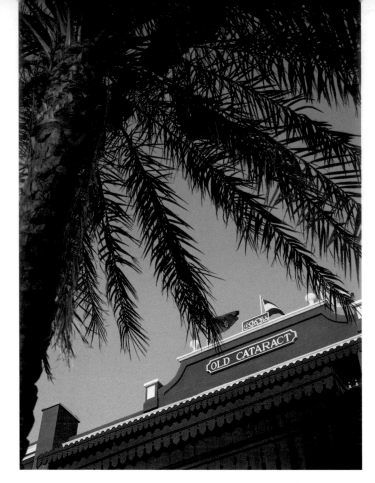

OLD CATARACT HOTEL, ASWAN

Wednesday

Well, this is the end. We are staying at the Old Cataract Hotel, which is under the same management (but nothing like as good) as the Winter Garden in Luxor. Spectacular views, though, and a really good street market. Lovely fresh produce, with incense burning on fruit stalls to keep the flies away. The artefacts are good, the produce is good, the traders are friendly and all we now have to do is endure the obligatory cruise up the Nile on a tacky old boat with organized trips and canteen catering and then, yippee, back to the only remaining civilized country in the Mediterranean, Spain!

below The elegant interiors of the Old Cataract Hotel.

PS. No wonder Agatha Christie was allegedly inspired to write *Death on the Nile* while staying at the Old Cataract Hotel.

Egypt, a Postscript

Egypt was the end of my journey around the Mediterranean and I ask myself what I have learned about Egyptian food. Well, the average Egyptian eats a lot of bread and the many varieties of Egyptian bread are some of the best in the world. Egyptian soups, the mainstay of the diet, are largely pulse-based – lentils, chickpeas, dried broad beans, etc. A dish of rice will be cooked in much the same way as in Spain, but more heavily flavoured with oriental spices such as caraway, cinnamon, cumin, saffron, turmeric and cardamom. The stews and casseroles are thicker, richer, spicier and sweeter and the use of fruit and nuts more prevalent than in the Western part of the Mediterranean. The influences of the Turks, the French and the Berbers, along with the effect of Cairo's geographical, and therefore trading, position in the world would be felt, from Asia to the East and Europe to the West, while the consequences of wars, conquests and trade and the unique fertility of the Nile valley have worked together to create a bizarre, exciting cuisine – sadly, now often found only in cookery books and on television screens. But, as Bo Diddley said in his famous song, you can't judge a book by looking at its cover.

index